MW00930025

Thank yu fo~ ~~~ ~~~~~~ ~

SEMPER FI

SSGT/USMC

Compliments of the Board of Doers & Team at
The Us4Warriors Foundation
Helping Warriors Past and
Present Live Stronger Lives
www.Us4Warriors.org

Thank you for your support.

DEMPSEY JSC

23/01/2022

A BATTLE WON BY HANDSHAKES

The Story of Alpha Company 1/5

LUCAS A. DYER

TRUE DIRECTIONS
AN AFFILIATE OF TARCHER BOOKS

A BATTLE WON BY HANDSHAKES
THE STORY OF ALPHA COMPANY 1/5

Copyright © 2014 Lucas A. Dyer.

All rights reserved. No part of this book may be used or reproduced by any means, graphic, electronic, or mechanical, including photocopying, recording, taping or by any information storage retrieval system without the written permission of the publisher except in the case of brief quotations embodied in critical articles and reviews.

iUniverse books may be ordered through booksellers or by contacting:

iUniverse LLC
1663 Liberty Drive
Bloomington, IN 47403
www.iuniverse.com
1-800-Authors (1-800-288-4677)

Because of the dynamic nature of the Internet, any web addresses or links contained in this book may have changed since publication and may no longer be valid. The views expressed in this work are solely those of the author and do not necessarily reflect the views of the publisher, and the publisher hereby disclaims any responsibility for them.

Any people depicted in stock imagery provided by Thinkstock are models, and such images are being used for illustrative purposes only. Certain stock imagery © Thinkstock.

ISBN: 978-1-4917-3200-7 (sc)
ISBN: 978-1-4917-3201-4 (hc)
ISBN: 978-1-4917-3198-7 (e)

Library of Congress Control Number: 2014906738

Printed in the United States of America.

iUniverse rev. date: 08/13/2014

The events that take place in this book are true stories from my own accounts and from those who served beside me in the Battle of Khanjar while participating in Operation Enduring Freedom in Helmand, Afghanistan, from May 2009 to December 2009.

May the stories told within be shared generously so that this part of history and those that gave the ultimate sacrifice not be forgotten. We demonstrated day by day, week by week, and month by month that a small, effective fighting force could unite with an Afghan people, become trusted and respected brothers-in-arms with their leaders and families, and make a difference in the US effort in Afghanistan. In doing so, we discovered what I believe to be the seed of enduring success in our AO.

This book is dedicated to the Marines of First Battalion Fifth Marines who gave the ultimate sacrifice so that you and I can sleep peacefully at night:

- Sergeant William Cahir, KIA August 13, 2009
- Lance Corporal Donald Hogan, KIA August 26, 2009
- Lance Corporal David R. Baker, KIA October 20, 2009
- Lance Corporal Justin J. Swanson, KIA November 10, 2009

For these men, duty, honor, and country are more than words; they are a way of life.

CONTENTS

PREFACE

The thoughts and ideas that I have put forward in this book are mine alone. Although I credit the Marine Corps and my leaders for the training I have received, and the trust of its commanders, nothing in this book reflects the ideas and thoughts of any other person or organization. I am not a professional writer, and I am not implying by writing this book that anyone has "got it wrong" or that I have all the right answers.

I started writing this book in January 2010, a few weeks after I came back from Helmand, Afghanistan. Many Marine Corps units have inserted and operated in this region, and much has changed since my return. It is an extremely difficult and elusive situation in Afghanistan. My book is about tactical employment of small, well-trained unit leaders that, when combined with a larger effort, has positive strategic implications. I am not here to imply that I think I could win the war in Afghanistan if put in charge, that I could meet these challenges alone, or that there are other units out there who could do it better. I just know what I have done, what I have learned, and what I would do again, if given the chance.

I was part of the Second MEB (Marine Expeditionary Brigade), which was commanded by Brigadier General Larry Nicholson. We were composed of approximately 4,000 Marines and 650 Afghan soldiers, along a seventy-five-mile stretch of the Helmand River south of Lashkar Gah.

ACKNOWLEDGMENTS

To the Marines and sailors of Alpha Company, First Battalion, Fifth Marines, Semper Fidelis, make peace or die! This book is for you so that you may share our story for years to come. To second squad, my squad of Marines who put all their confidence in me that I would bring them home alive, or die trying.

To my platoon, first platoon, which trusted in my ability to command and lead them as their platoon commander. Both gave it their all day in and day out for seven months straight in an unconventional war where each day could have been our last. They never doubted me and charged with smiles on their faces every time.

A special thanks to photographer, Lucian Read, whom was embedded with our company for the initial assault into Nawa. His photos will help the longevity of this story to live on and become a part of history. I could not have done this without the generous support and dedication of Karla Sharke, Christopher Aher, Dave Olson, Myji-Ryan Photography, Jonathan Glover, Gordon Guyant, Adrian Pouchoulen, Kyle Rodgers, Bobby McHugh, Stan, Gerri, Kylee, and Lauren Spooner, James Amos, Jonathan Stiner, Steve and Sandy Lieberman, Rick Alan Denning, and the San Clemente Marine Corps Support Group. Also to Frank Denault and his brothers of Third Battalion, Fifth Marines.

Lastly, to the Marines who could not make it back home with us. You will never be forgotten, and your stories of heroism live on through us in hopes that one day your children will read about you and all that you sacrificed for this country. RIP, fellow brothers.

THE SECRETARY OF THE NAVY

The President of the United States takes pleasure in presenting the PRESIDENTIAL UNIT CITATION to

MARINE EXPEDITIONARY BRIGADE-AFGHANISTAN

for service as set forth in the following

CITATION:

For outstanding performance in action against enemy forces from 29 May 2009 to 12 April 2010, in support of Operation ENDURING FREEDOM. Marine Expeditionary Brigade-Afghanistan conducted the most holistic counterinsurgency campaign since the Coalition presence in Afghanistan began in 2001. Operating in three separate and austere provinces that had been bereft of government efficacy for years, the Brigade constructed expeditionary bases and air fields, and struck decisively at the heart of the Taliban insurgency with Operation KHANJAR in July 2009. Cities and hamlets across the region, from Now Zad to Khan Neshin, resumed regional commerce and schooling for children, and participated in national elections. Concurrent with kinetic fighting, the Brigade engaged tribal, religious, and government leaders with population-centric civil-military operations that synchronized developmental efforts across 58,000 square miles of battle-space. In February 2010, Operation MOSHTARAK reclaimed Marjah, a strategic agricultural hub and narco-terrorist safe haven in the Helmand River Valley. Together with thousands of Afghan National Security Forces, the Brigade tangibly improved the geo-political landscape of Southwestern Afghanistan. By their outstanding courage, aggressive fighting spirit, and untiring devotion to duty, the officers, enlisted personnel, and civilian employees of Marine Expeditionary Brigade-Afghanistan reflected great credit upon themselves and upheld the highest traditions of the Marine Corps and the United States Naval Service.

For the President,

Secretary of the Navy

Secretary of Navy Letter

CHAPTER I

THE LARGEST HELO-BORNE AIRLIFT INSERT SINCE VIETNAM

If we're not successful here, you'll have a staging base for global terrorism all over the world. People will say the terrorists won. And you'll see expressions of these kinds of things in Africa, South America, you name it. Any developing country is going to say, this is the way we beat [the United States], and we're going to have a bigger problem. A setback or loss for the United States would be a tremendous boost for jihadist extremists, fundamentalists all over the world and provide a global infusion of morale and energy, and these people don't need much.
—Bob Woodward, *Obama's Wars*

July 2, 2009

The day had finally arrived when all of the training leading up to this deployment, and all the extra training we had put in at Camp Leatherneck, would pay off. I have always said that combat for an infantry Marine is our Super Bowl. There are no other opportunities for us to test our skills in a real-world manner like there is in combat. I often discourage the sports/Marine analogy because one is for fun, and the other is life or death. However, in this case, the bottom line is that combat is our main event.

We all had worked extremely hard for this and were beyond eager to have our infantry skills put to the test. The information on the exact time of the launch was kept quiet, and nobody knew the exact details. Months out, we knew we were going into Afghanistan, specifically Helmand Province. Weeks out, we knew we were inserting via helicopters, CH-53E (or commonly called a "bird") from Camp Bastion somewhere south. Days out, we knew we were leaving sometime in the first week of July, and twenty-four hours prior, we were confined to our company area as a battalion for one final formation. This formation was held by the Second Marine Expeditionary Brigade (MEB) Sergeant Major Ernest Hoopii.

The battalion had gathered around in one big circle, and it was dark; the only lights were those that lit up at night around Leatherneck. Some of us couldn't see much, but we could make out a tall figure with a pistol across his body. Marines were quiet, eagerly awaiting the final motivational speech commonly associated with the last few hours before crossing into the shit.

"Marines," he yelled. "Are you ready to kick some Taliban ass?"

We all cheered back, "Ooh-rah!"

The sound of one thousand plus Marines echoed all through Leatherneck. We were so loud that I think the enemy heard us down in Nawa. We were so loud we most likely disturbed the POGs (persons other than a grunt) who were sound asleep, complaining on Facebook that Leatherneck was rough and dangerous, or bitching because the chow hall had run out of ice cream.

"That's freaking outstanding because here in a few hours, you are going to insert behind enemy lines and put your skills to the test!" Sergeant Major Hoopii continued to yell so we all could hear him. "Gentlemen, shortly you will stand where no Marine has ever stood!" He pointed south in the direction of Nawa. "So button your chinstraps, and let's do what Marines do!" He looked around at us all as we cheered and screamed "Ooh-rah," "Errrrr," "E-Tool," "Kill," and other little nonsense sounds Marines make, which only Marines understand. "Know that tonight, before you jump on that bird, the enemy is waiting. The enemy is ready, and the enemy is praying to his god. I highly suggest you do the same to show them our God is more powerful. I want you to grab your rifle, hold it high above your head, and shout their god's name so he knows we are coming! *Allah Akbar! Allah Akbar! Allah Akbar!*"

I must admit it did feel a little awkward yelling *"Allah Akbar."* I had never really said it before. I would never have had a reason to yell it, let alone say it, but it felt good hearing the roaring sound travel from all of us war-hungry Marines, rifles in the air, waving our arms around like the terrorists did on TV. I felt for a brief moment as if I was literately screaming at their god, showing him that we were not scared and ready for battle. Sergeant Major Hoopii proceeded to tell us how proud and honored he was to be led by such fine Marines with such great reputations and wished us luck.

After the formation, we were all dismissed to our respective companies and fell out into our staging area next to our company tent. Our packs were all covered down and aligned, looking sharp; a few glowing flashlights were moving about as Marines looked for last-minute items, followed by some chatter and laughs.

For the most part, the majority of us were quiet. We had already called home to our family and said our good-byes or "talk to you when I can next." There wasn't much more to say really, and we were not exactly sure when we would have the opportunity to make another phone call. All we knew was that for five to seven days, we were surviving off what we packed. No resupplies of any kind. From there, it would take at least a month, according to Captain Day, our company commander, to establish a permanent operating post. I was actually prepared to not call home for seven months; letters were fine.

On Wednesday night, we arrived at Camp Bastion around 1800 and immediately went over to our staging area. We organized into manifest sticks of twenty-one Marines in each manifest per bird. Sitting on the flight line, which was the final staging area before we took off and inserted into Nawa, we talked about sports, told stories of all the wild times we had, and just enjoyed the final hours. We didn't talk about the battle we would soon be in. We didn't glorify firefights or speculate about how many kills we were going to have. There was no need since our level of professionalism was beyond that. Every Marine knew this was not going to be won by attrition warfare, which doctrinally in the Marine Corps means victory through the cumulative destruction of the enemy by capturing terrain and killing them and to overwhelm the enemy through sheer force. We were told by many that this insert would be the largest helicopter insert since Vietnam. Knowing that Vietnam was a large insert, it was difficult for me to truly appreciate and understand exactly how big it was going to be until the final piece of the planning came together.

The sounds of helicopters started to fade in from the night sky. Small blinking lights started to appear in a long row flying toward us. The CH-53s started to come in one after another, landing on the flight line, which seemed to stretch a mile. As one would land, so would another, then another, and then another until the runway was filled. It was then that it all became reality and hit home. The stated purpose directed down by International Security Assistance Force (ISAF), the mission, the planning, and the long hours all hit at once. I finally realized that Alpha Company 1/5 was officially part of President Barack Obama's twenty-one-thousand-troop surge into

Afghanistan, and I finally understood the concept of exactly how large this air assault was.

Our stick strapped up and moved out toward the tarmac in a single-file line. We headed toward the back of the ramp, which was lowered for us. There was so much downwind coming from the rotors that when I got within fifteen feet, I was forced back. The intense rotor wash in the already hot climate felt like I was walking into an oven. To make for an even more unpleasant situation, I had to take a knee just short of the ramp to count my Marines as they loaded up. 1, 2, 3, 4, 5.

It was quite painful stepping up onto the bird, and the back of my neck and face suddenly felt like they were on fire. I peeled up onto the ramp and sat down right next to the door gunner as the ramp closed. I looked around, gave a thumbs-up, and everyone replied back with thumbs-ups. Just prior to inserting, we would go completely blacked out, using only our night vision goggles (NVGs) and natural light from the moon. The bird began to lift off into the dark Afghanistan night.

We all knew the flight would be about thirty minutes, but we were unsure of what we would be expecting as the helicopter landed. Of course, we prepared for enemy contact at the landing zone (LZ) just in case we did take small arms fire (SAF).

I was looking out the back down at the ground from the bird, and for the first time, I saw the actual layout of the environment we would be operating on. You could prepare all you wanted by looking at a map and photos, but nothing was better than seeing it firsthand.

Our platoon sergeant, Staff Sergeant O'Brian, was sitting across from me. We both noticed a string of waterways running all over the ground. The canals ran in every which way, ranging in depth from waist-high to over our heads. It looked like a topographical view of a major city's highways. We both looked up at one another.

"Hey, Dyer. Do you see that?" He pointed down at the canals.

"Yeah. They look completely different than what we planned for!" I yelled back, trying to scream over the sound of the bird.

Behind us, there were helicopters as far as the eye could see at night. It was surreal to be a part of this organization that was minutes away from inserting deep into enemy territory. The sky was clear, and the moon was almost full. The light illuminated the ground and shimmered off the canals. It was fascinating to see, knowing that in just a few minutes, we would be stepping foot on that very ground.

The one minute out from insert mark came. The crew chief signaled to us with his pointer finger. One minute. Everybody looked around, acknowledging the sign.

Our NVGs went down, and we took a few deep breaths. My heart rate started to increase a little, and it got even more surreal. As the bird started to descend, making its way toward the LZ, I was anticipating at anytime a massive amount of enemy fire engaging us in an attempt to shoot us down.

Our bird touched down with ease; there appeared to be no sounds of gunfire. The gate dropped, and I was the first to exit, taking an immediate knee outside the ramp. I counted the Marines off—1, 2, 3, 4—ensuring that we all exited. We had practiced exiting the bird over and over, but a few Marines still found it possible to fall face-first off the gate.

With my NVGs on, and all personnel off the bird, the pilot got the thumbs-up and took off. The morning had never seemed as quiet as it did once the helicopters took off. We were alone with just the gear on our backs and Marines to our left and to our right.

I took my squad to our preplanned spot, making up the twelve o'clock to four o'clock sector of our 360-degree security, or covering the north to east sector. I didn't allow anyone to sleep and kept us at

100 percent; I constantly walked the lines to ensure that my squad was up and alert.

It was two o'clock in the morning, dead silent, and several helicopters had just touched down, inserting hundreds of Marines in the middle of someone's backyard. With that amount of noise, two thoughts were going through my head: Either the enemy had seen us and had started to set up an ambush—or they had gotten scared and ran. As the sun started to rise, we were about to find out.

CHAPTER II

A DOCTRINAL APPROACH TO OPERATION KHANJAR

It's certainly a clash of civilizations. It's a clash of
religions. It's a clash of almost concepts of how to live.
The conflict is that deep, so I think if you don't succeed
in Afghanistan, you will be fighting in more places.
—Bob Woodward, *Obama's Wars*

In early summer of 2009, our commander in chief, President Barack
Obama ordered approximately twenty-one thousand troops to deploy
to Afghanistan. As part of this group, I was first to arrive, heading
directly to Helmand Province with the Second MEB to launch
Operation Khanjar, also called Operation Strike of the Sword. We
were told we would be forging new ground and going to places
Marines have never been. Our combined mission was to provide
security for population centers along the Helmand River Valley and
connect local citizens with their legitimate government, to establish
stable and secure conditions for national elections scheduled for
August, and to enhance security for the future.

The vision as I saw it was more general: To create a zone of
security, economic activity, and increased freedom of movement

for the majority of the region's most populated areas within our area of operations (AO). Up until that point, the Taliban fighters had essentially encircled the district of Nawa and Lashkar Gah, launching several daring raids to destabilize the provincial capital. The Taliban insurgency virtually controlled the Helmand River Valley, including key populated districts and towns—from Nawa all the way up north to Kajaki and Musa Qala.

Within our AO, Taliban fighters and narcotics traffickers maintained operational support zones throughout. Insurgents began terrorizing the local bazaars, levying taxes on merchants, and seeding the roads with improvised explosive devices (IEDs). Shopkeepers placed their merchandises behind padlocked tin doors, teachers closed the schools, doctors abandoned the health clinics, and a majority of all the local nationals fled. In general, the insurgents would transit through the Pakistani border and desert until they reached Khan Neshin, which served as the first contact point for insurgents moving north. There, fighters would seek shelter, food, and supplies, such as weapons and IED materials, before making their way back into Nawa to attack coalition forces.

As a small unit leader, I was given a great deal of trust and responsibilities that far exceeded my peers who were working in the civilian sectors. Age at that point becomes minimally important as it truly is just a number. The responsibilities, although different, share a need for mission accomplishment. Our mission was accomplished by understanding the three levels of war (tactical, operational, and strategic) and incorporating many tangible variables. Our training was focused on understanding how all of our actions at the tactical level, which is the lowest level of war, have both positive and negative implications at the strategic level—the highest level of war. It was crucial that we all understood this, and even more important was understanding the not-so-sexy doctrinal approach to combat.

In the planning, development, and training process, we had to incorporate joint-effort scenarios so that we could work within the guidelines that NATO and ISAF had planned. This later came into play when we partnered with Afghan counterparts in a joint effort.

At first glance, training for combat seems relatively simple. If you see bad guys, shoot the bad guys. If bad guys see you and shoot, simply shoot, move, and communicate. The infantry has been doing this since the dawn of the Marine Corps: To locate, close with, and destroy the enemy by fire and maneuver and repel the enemy's assault by fire and close combat. But when the pages are turned and the layers of the onion are peeled back, there is more to combat than aiming a firearm and shooting, especially in nonconventional combat when you can't always distinguish between friend and foe.

You have to be just as quick to lend a helping hand as you are to pull the trigger. Tactics change, techniques change, and procedures adjust to meet the demands of the battlefield. As you will read in another chapter, winning this war and coming out successful in our AO was a challenge. It took more than just maneuvering on the enemy and capturing terrain. Understanding the doctrinal aspect was a key element for us.

We wanted to go to war with a guerilla-style, unconventional enemy, and we didn't really care about long-term strategic goals. Killing the enemy in Afghanistan was like swatting mosquitos; you kill one, and a hundred come to the funeral angry. So we had to look at this seven-month deployment with short-term *and* long-term objectives.

Counterinsurgency Operations (COIN) are defined as military, paramilitary, political, economic, psychological, and civic actions taken by a government to defeat an insurgency (DOD-MCWP 3-33.5). How would we implement a COIN methodology into this? Understanding counterinsurgency from a doctrinal approach was a start. The higher-up or strategic political power is the central issue in insurgencies and counterinsurgencies. Planning is organized and executed around population-focused operations.

This was conducted by adopting ASCOPE and looking at it from the local national's perspective (ASCOPE: Area, Structure, Capabilities, Organization, People, Event). ASCOPE is one of the best ways to teach the small unit leader how to fully understand the terrain (human and physical) within the COIN environment. ASCOPE is a great concept to use—as long as it is being utilized as the main task and not a secondary or tertiary task while conducting a patrol.

Conventional doctrine reminds us that there are two classifications as they relate to the mission while on a patrol: reconnaissance and combat. Reconnaissance patrols gather information about the enemy, terrain, or resources. Relying on stealth rather than combat strength allowed us to gather information and fight only when necessary to complete the mission or to defend ourselves.

The distance covered by reconnaissance patrols varied based on the terrain and mission. Our squad was ideally suited for reconnaissance patrol missions because of its relative small size and its experience of working together. A combat patrol, on the other hand, is a fighting, patrol-assigned mission that required engagement with the enemy in combat—we liked those!

Larger and more heavily armed than reconnaissance patrols, combat patrols had a mission to capture enemy documents, provide security, and capture or destroy enemy equipment and installations. Such action was ordinarily followed by a return to friendly positions. Regardless of the mission, we were required to report any information concerning the enemy and terrain acquired during the accomplishment of the assigned mission.

Although ASCOPE was often issued as the mission and executed as the type of patrol, there were only four types of combat patrols: raid, contact, ambush, and security (normally conducted by a Marine rifle platoon). A rifle platoon reinforced with crew-served weapons such as light and medium machine guns was normally considered the minimum size for contact, economy of force, or ambush patrols.

In some situations, such as the capture of a small enemy outpost, a rifle platoon could conduct a raid. However, raids were complex missions; due to the organization of a raid force (command, reconnaissance, assault, support, security, and reserve elements), a rifle company was normally the smallest force assigned to a raid.

ASCOPE missions ensured that "key terrain" to the population became key terrain for us as the ground-holding or embedded unit. What we considered important was often not what the population thought was important. Similarly, we could use that tool while partnered with Afghan partners. The information built over time as each patrol amended, enhanced, and "downloaded" the information gathered after each patrol. We duped all the data associated with our specific target area in order to build our S2 databases.

The end state of ASCOPE was the Commander's Critical Information Requirements (CCIR) for future patrols that were related to areas that were important to the population and our AO. For more on this, refer to "Lessons Learned at the Strategic and Tactical Levels."

Enemy Focus-Tactics	Population Focus-Tactics
▪ **Environment**	▪ **Environment**
-Enemy is foreign, or local influence; ideologically, ethnically, religiously, culturally separated from people	-Fighters mostly local; related to elders and/or villagers
-Enemy is unwanted in AO	-Traditional society where elders are "local government
-Popular desire for kill/capture open to population	-Little poplar desire for kill/capture; popular tolerance for fighters as individuals
-People are connected with gov't	-Immature environment; economic deprivation; fractured society
-Developed AO: enemy disrupts economy, functional activities of daily life	-Little connection with central gov't
▪ **Techniques**	▪ **Techniques**
-Focus on kill/capture w/lethal and non-lethal methods.	-Marginalize and isolate insurgent leaders via focus on strengthening traditional leaders, governance, jobs, and developments. Lethal and non-lethal apply
-Target HVI, HVTs, and CCIRs	
-Other methods as needed.	-Kill/capture isolated enemy after deliberately setting conditions

Determining the Appropriate Strategy Utilizing ASCOPE

When a mission was given involving ASCOPE it felt doctrinally wrong because it read: *Conduct an ASCOPE patrol in vicinity of (IVO) of "insert any one of our hundreds of locations" in order to gather information for the S2 database. Be prepared to (BPT) confirm or deny any enemy activity in our AO. Mission has priority.*

As a squad leader, how do you task organize your elements when you are going against everything you were ever taught? How do you conduct an ASCOPE patrol? You do it by breaking free of structured information and incorporating new concepts directed by those higher. You trust your commanders to know what they are doing. We called this the 1/5 Victory Mind-set.

1. Be a combat hunter—own your environment.

2. Perform every task to standard—every time.
3. Account for your people and equipment—always.
4. Identify and work through local leaders (local government, tribal, ANSF, mullahs, etc.).
5. Build trust with the Afghans we live among.
6. Never promise what you can't immediately deliver.
7. Exercise tactical patience—control the action/reaction cycle.
8. Ruthlessly enforce standards and PCIs/PCCs.
9. Do what you know is right.
10. Solve problems with the assets at hand.

We also utilized acronyms such as TCAPF: Tactical Conflict Assessment & Planning Framework. This was decentralized from higher and executed at the tactical level by the small unit leader. This set us up for Conflict Assessment Framework (CAF) (Strategic & Operational Levels).

The intent and purpose for using these two methods is to compliment ASCOPE and assist in the creation and stabilization of plans toward stability within an area by eliminating grievances by the key local nationals. It was important to find their means and motivation, opportunity of vulnerability, and resiliencies and capitalize on every window of opportunity which brought us closer to gaining their trust. The method uses basic questions from the squad leader, and any local national can be interviewed—not just key leaders. The questions were designed to get to the root causes of instability, not just the surface. We would aggregate these answers locally, and work by, with, and through the Afghan government to solve the problems at the higher level. I would sort out which information would benefit the higher level and which information would be kept for us for future missions.

COIN is and has been a successful strategy that has been used for years in our military. The concept was new to us, but after utilizing this method for seven months, I established that there were three levels to control in COIN:

1. Providing constant security: Control the tempo by the use of military and ANSF attachments as well as local police (ANP, ANCOP). The goal is for both local and national security once we hand it over to them.

2. Political goals: Limit and control the violence by ensuring the political agenda is being met. Ask yourself if the success is going to bring political restrictions or if the failure is due to political restrictions, How are we disturbing the dynamic's power to the people?

3. Stabilize any economic growth made. Control the stability by developing spending habits to boost profit. Use in-house humanitarian assistance by handing out radios, food, water, and clothes. Work with civil affairs and higher to help fund, build, and accelerate resources and infrastructure management (roads, water supply, sewers, living conditions, etc.).

Partnering with Afghan counterparts was another nondoctrinal approach that we took. I have read many MCDP and MCWP publications in my time, but none of them prepared me for working with the ANA, ANP, and ANCOP. The ANA were the Afghan National Army, the main branch of the Afghan Armed Forces who were responsible for ground elements. The unit we had assigned to us was the 215th Corps, which partnered with the Marine Expeditionary Brigade in Helmand.

The ANA were hard to work with from a tactical perspective. We had a good group, and they were always willing to go with us on patrols and never gave too much resistance. They were energetic and hated the enemy more than we did. They were great to enter buildings and compounds with and served as a vital part of us gaining the trust of local nationals. However, when it came to them shooting or isolating the enemy, they were pretty much worthless.

The ANP were the Afghan National Police, which was the primary police force of Afghanistan. They serve as the single law enforcement agency in all of Afghanistan. I always felt the ANP were corrupt, and I didn't trust them or rely on them to get a whole lot done. The ANA didn't like them, and the ANP didn't like the ANA—it was always a great time working together!

The last group we partnered with occasionally was ANCOP. The Afghan National Civil Order Police was a step above the regular ANP and were a branch of the ANP force. They were a newer organization, set up around 2006, and provided civil order presence patrols and maintained peace by preventing violent public incidents. Their intimidation factor was great to have while conducting raids or hard hits. We didn't patrol with them as much as we did the ANA; we mostly used the ANP and ANCOP to meet us at given locations when conducting personnel and house searches using raids, hard hits, cordons and searches, or cordon and knocks.

I felt that in order to gauge success in this intense, unconventional, complex war, I would have to be able to walk through a marketplace or a down a street and see open shops that were selling goods and services. There would have to be a flow of commerce, a recognizable and functioning government, and functional schools and hospitals.

CHAPTER III

ALL IN A DAY'S WORK

We have killed thousands and thousands of the "enemy"
in Afghanistan, and it clearly has not brought us closer
to our objectives there. We could kill thousands more
and still not be any closer five years from now.
—Major Jim Gant, United States Army Special Forces

Dawn came quickly, and we got no sleep. Everybody had stayed up on high alert since the insert, waiting for the sun to break so we could step off on our first movement in Nawa. We knew that we would be on our own with limited supplies for the next four to five days. The gear we had packed on our bodies was the gear we were living with over the next week. At that point, we planned to establish an area we could use and start to establish a place to operate out of. From our insert point, we had an approximate 14 x 5 click area to cover. This is roughly fourteen thousand meters by five thousand meters of unknown area that we had to cover and move through.

On the morning of July 2, my squad was moving north toward a suspected enemy bazaar. My squad's mission was to set up an inner cordon in order to allow second squad, led by Corporal Pouchoulen (Pancho), to search the compound and surrounding area. Corporal

Hoard (Rocky) was the third squad leader and was the far squad to the west. His mission was to provide the outer cordon. Attached to me, I had one sniper team with three Marines: a team leader, a shooter, and his spotter. I had worked before with the team leader, Sergeant Pongo, and I knew that if anything needed to get done, he was the Marine for the job. Sergeant Pongo was an interesting Marine; if you met him, you would have never guessed he was a reservist. There was an active duty versus reservist stigma, and you could usually tell when someone was a reservist—or so it always seemed. We were just different than they were.

Our platoon was pretty much online, sweeping and searching every compound, haystack, vehicle, and person we came across in hopes of finding weapons, drugs, contraband, or anything worthwhile to gather for intelligence. We also kept an eye out for the enemy. We were moving slowly and methodically, utilizing bounding over watch and satellite patrolling. One team would move into a covered or concealed position and provide security as another team moved forward. Because of the intense heat, we would move tree line-to-tree line, using whatever shade we could find. The heat index alone in July was 115 to 125 degrees Fahrenheit during the day, and the sixty-plus pounds of gear easily made it feel like 135 degrees.

Within the first hour, we received sporadic small arms fire from our west. The ANA attached with us, which was controlled by the British, returned fire along with a few from third squad. This lasted for about twenty minutes, but it did not really slow us down. It did make us wonder exactly what they were shooting at.

The sound of gunfire was startling at first. The snap sound associated with it is scary, but I suppose it was good news when the shot was heard since I would imagine you don't hear the shot that kills you. The movement from our insert point up to that point was quiet for the most part. The only consistency I could pick up on was that different villages appeared to have boundary lines, and once we crossed them, small arms fire would break out. Other than that, it was a lot of attempting to talk to local nationals. At that point, having someone talk to us was more of a challenge than dodging sporadic small arms fire. The platoon decided to take a small security halt in order to look around the area. This type of security halt is often referred by us infantry guys as SLLS (stop, look, listen, smell). Many of my noninfantry friends call it SEALS (stop, eat, and let's sleep). The purpose of SLLS is to slow the pace down, take a short tactical pause, and look around the battlefield.

My squad at the time was up on a small hilltop that was a cemetery. Most cemeteries in our AO were the only pieces of elevated ground we could find. From our position, we could not see any enemies—or anyone who appeared to be shooting at us—but we could clearly hear the gunfire. The terrain was flat and dry. The fields had all been tilled by tractors in preparation for flooding so they could have good irrigation when they started to grow corn in late July.

They had just finished the poppy season, and everything had been cut down and harvested. This made patrolling across fields very challenging for several reasons. It left us vulnerable and wide open with no cover, and the unstable, uneven ground was extremely difficult to walk on. There were tree lines between our squads, but the skinny trees offered little protection from the sun. Running in the middle of these tree lines were small canals that were about two to four feet in depth and about five feet wide. Small man-made mud bridges helped us cross them, but we stayed away from them more then we used them in case they were rigged with IEDs.

As we moved north, the platoon commander, Second Lieutenant Barhugesen (Bart), found an empty compound and wanted to meet up to go firm for a small period of time. Going firm was a way to take a small tactical pause in the operation in order to look at the mission and discuss our next move. It was like a football huddle to go over the next plays and ensure that everyone was on the same page.

As my squad came within about two hundred meters, all that separated us from the compound was an open field. We opened up our dispersion to about fifteen meters between one another, and bounded one fire team at a time. I went across with Corporal Camacho, my first fire team leader, and as soon as we stepped off, we received some small arms fire. Since the shots seemed more to our west, just as before, we quickly crossed the field toward the compound.

Corporal Hoard's squad was north of our position about a thousand meters (one click), and he was not going to come back to meet up. I took my squad and moved into the compound, posting out security as I went in to meet with the platoon commander. I went over the map with the platoon commander and Corporal Pancho to confirm our next objective and do our last-minute checks before we moved in.

Rocky's squad didn't have to come back and meet us because his objective was to move ahead of the platoon and set up the outer cordon while my squad followed right behind. My squad was tasked with setting up the inner cordon while second squad was going to search the suspected enemy bazaar.

When we came up to the objective, I placed my squad on the far side of a little canal, in the tree line that faced into the compound. I put one fire team to our rear to cover us and a Marine on each end to turn outboard to protect our flanks.

Corporal Pancho called to say he would take the north side of the compound and asked if we could search the south side. The compound seemed large enough for us to do so without fear of blue on blue; a term we use when talking about shooting at each other. It was a lot bigger than we had suspected and what we perceived from our maps. So I took two Marines and my Afghanistan interpreter (terp) Ali, who I nicknamed Jimmy. He was attached to me for this whole deployment to help translate, across the canal and into the compound.

Given the movement over the last few hours and the sporadic small arms fire to our west, things were heating up. The compound we were about to enter was the start of a small village that we had to go through in order to get to Marjah Kalay, which was the first objective for the day. The immediate area was pretty quiet, given what had just happened. It was textbook in saying that something didn't feel right, but we could not put our fingers on it.

We entered from the back—or what we believed to be the back. At the time, we were unsure. Some of these compounds were like huge mazes. They looked the same from all angles. We searched one section of it, which looked like a compound within a compound. It was like a series of apartment buildings attached to one another inside a giant fenced-in area. The fence and the rest of the compound were made of mud.

One section had a few cows and some chickens on the inside, which we soon learned was the norm. We did not run into any local nationals living in that particular compound. Maybe they happened to be gone that day—or maybe they ran away. It was possible that someone had warned them to get out, leaving only Taliban behind.

I was not sure at that point, but the area was very quiet. It seemed odd since it looked like the perfect setting for something to go wrong. We had seen very few local nationals; out of the ones we did see, only a handful actually talked to us. As soon as we entered the village, the small arms fire stopped. We continued to search that part of the compound and found nothing.

Our searches were very different than typical searches. We were not law enforcement, and we didn't carry search warrants. If I wanted to look at something, I looked. If something looked out of place or suspicious, I looked into it. It was more of look under, over, around, in, and behind everything.

After spending about thirty minutes searching, we came up short. Nothing exciting, but I wasn't really sure what we were going to find anyway. We had been briefed for any possibility—hidden treasure, gold, a stash of Afghan money, weapons, anticoalition propaganda, maybe even a real-life Taliban or drugs.

I called over the radio and told my fire team leaders to exit and decided to start on the next compound. We exited and went to another one. In the adjacent compound, we found nobody. It was odd since it was supposed to be an enemy bazaar, and it really was just a giant compound.

We went back outside and moved over to the next building, which was a mosque. As we walked up to the entrance, a male local national walked out with a brown dress, dark hair, and a clean shave. Our terp came over, and we started asking him questions. I looked at the individual as if we were in a real face-to-face conversation. My terp would listen to me talking to him and then translate it for the individual.

Whenever I met people, I wanted to get a few demographics about them. I would ask for a full name, age, and which village they lived in. Are you part of a tribe? What is the name of the tribe? Who is your village elder? I would go into other questions, such as if they knew who we were? Do you know why we are here? Do you feel safe? Are there any threats in the area we should know about? It was similar to being questioned by the police.

This local national was in his early twenties, and he claimed to live in the compound. He said his name was Mohammed Gul. We searched him and asked him several questions about this place. We talked to him about the area we had searched, the whereabouts of the villagers, and why we were receiving small arms fire.

He didn't know much, but he was cooperative—and even offered us water from his well. He let us search the inside of his compound and the mosque. It looked like every other place we had searched. As we were walking out, I noticed a small alley with the entrance blocked by sheets. It looked like there was another room at the end of the alley. I asked him what it was, and he said it was another house. When I asked who lived there, he told me he did. It was all his; he lived in this giant compound. It felt strange, and we all went over to check it out.

At that point, we had been in the area for a little over an hour. Nothing had come up, and I was going to take one last look before we moved on. My instincts were right. There was another room, and inside the room was a small building with four local nationals hiding in it. There were two males—a father in his fifties and a son in his twenties. The two females were their wives. We asked them questions about themselves and if they knew a Mohammed Gul.

I would always ask other people if they knew certain names to verify that the names we were given were correct. The younger individual had a large sum of money in his shirt pocket. At least it was larger than what most had from what we had seen that day. At that point, all I could do was ask him about what he did, where he got the money, and why he had it. All questions were answered reasonably. Nothing seemed too suspicious—other than that they said they did not know Mohammed Gul, and Mohammed Gul said he did not know them, even though he had claimed to live there ten minutes earlier. Both parties claimed not to know anyone who lived in the compound, other than their families.

It was a lot to take in. I was confused beyond belief. No crimes were being committed. No drugs, no weapons, and no hostile act or intent. It was just a family and one male who claimed to own the whole compound, but there was a family of four living in another building inside his compound, and he did not know them—and they did not know him. We filled up on water, thanked him for his time, and started off. And that's when it got weird.

As we were picking up to leave, one of the snipers spotted a male local national watching us from behind the far southern wall. As I moved toward him, he ran away. I ran over to his spot, but he had vanished. I looked around for a few minutes without seeing anybody.

I made the call to pick up and move. The squad got up, my terp and I walked together along the compound wall, on line with Lance Corporal Stoner who was point man in first fire team. The rest of the squad patrolled on the other side of a small canal that was about two feet deep and three to four feet wide. The compound wall ended and opened up into a giant field. Past the wall, we had no more cover.

I halted the squad, took a knee, and used my rifle scope to look around. I didn't see anything. It was very quiet, and I felt like we were being watched, but I couldn't see anyone. For some reason, I stopped and took out my camera to take a picture. It was a good photo to show how open our AO was. There was a large field before the next series of compounds. Just as I raised the camera to my face, a loud, cracking burst of machine gun fire impacted inches above my head on the wall beside me. The dirt on the wall shattered off, spraying all over me. In the same second, more rounds hit the deck just in front of me. The squad was taking heavy machine gun fire from two different directions. We were surrounded; it appeared that we had walked directly into an ambush.

The whole time we were patrolling up to this village, the Taliban had been setting up their first defensive position. Just as this started, second squad and third squad came under attack as well. It was a well-planned ambush which we had to fight our way out. In a matter of seconds, the entire platoon came under attack from multiple locations and multiple compounds. They had been waiting for us, knowing that we would come through the village.

I quickly dropped to the deck, and my terp did too. He was grabbing my leg and begging them not to kill him. He yelled, "Please, Sergeant Dyer, don't let them kill me! Please help me!"

I immediately turned and yelled to Corporal Camacho, "Hey! Move your team into the canal for some cover, and have Corporal Jefferson set up the 240. And get rounds downrange!"

Sergeant Pongo had already set up his Marines and was sending rounds downrange with the M40 at an enemy machine position. I looked around to assess the situation and realized we were in a pretty shitty spot. If we moved in any direction, we would expose ourselves to more fire. I wouldn't say we were pinned down because being pinned down is a state of mind. Nothing was physically holding us there, but we were in a tight spot.

Instantly, my mind started playing out scenarios and going through options. I refer to these options as my tactics, techniques, and procedures (TTPs). It seemed to take a long time, but it all played out in a matter of seconds. A decision had to be made, or lives would be lost—and losing Marines is never an option.

I went with my instincts and relied on my years of training. My fire teams were maneuvering, the 240B machine gun was suppressing the enemy, and the snipers were taking precision shots at the targets they could see. I had two radio channels going at once, one to the adjacent squad leaders and one to the platoon commander. I was doing my best to send in the initial contact report and keep them informed so we didn't fire at each other.

The rate of fire picked up from the enemy, and all I could hear was loud cracking all around us. The rounds were impacting so close that I was actually waiting to get hit. I knew it would happen, but I wasn't sure exactly when. The shots were creeping in on us, and the accuracy was improving.

I rolled to a different channel and decided to use our supporting arms. I told my terp to grab my radio from my pouch. He and I had rehearsed this hundreds of times. All my radio channels were preprogramed so I could switch back and forth talking to whom I needed to, when I needed to from intersquad, second and third squad, platoon commander, Company net, 81 mortar platoon, and artillery. I felt my gear moving a little bit, and I thought he was getting my radio. Suddenly over my right shoulder his hand popped out with a package of Band-Aids from my individual first-aid kit (IFAK). I think he misunderstood what I was asking. "My fucking radio, man! Not Band-Aids!"

He did it right, and I was now talking to the 81s on their fire net and I started my fire mission. This happened within seconds, but it seemed like it was taking forever. I called in my fire transmission. "Mohawk, this is Apache 2-1, stand by for POSREP over." POSREP was my position report to let them know where I was currently positioned.

"Apache 2-1, this is Mohawk. Standing by for POSREP. Out."

"Apache 2-1 is currently located at grid 41RPQ2060-6521. Over."

"Roger. Mohawk copies grid 41RPQ2060-6521. Out."

"Mohawk, adjust fire polar. Over."

"Adjust fire polar. Out."

"Direction, 0040 break, distance three hundred, danger close. Over."

"Mohawk copies direction, 0040 break, distance three hundred, requesting danger close. Out."

Right before I started the next transmission, one of the Marines yelled, "RPG! Take cover!"

Before I even knew what was happening, an RPG went directly over my head, impacting on the wall behind me. The RPG exploded a few feet above my head, knocking me down and covering me with dirt and debris. Within a second, another one impacted just short of Corporal Jefferson and his gunner on the 240B. The RPG blew up the small section of wall, covering Jefferson's face and blowing the wall into pieces. He was knocked back into the canal, and I was sure he'd been hit. It was just way too close. It turned out that the son of bitch survived untouched and had a little ear ringing.

Just as that happened, Corporal Bounds fired back with a light antiarmor weapon (LAAW), impacting right where they had shot the RPG from. For about ten seconds, the enemy fire halted, but then it picked right back up again.

"Taking heavy machine gun and RPG fire from a six-man element inside a compound. GRG J3F, buildings 65, 73, and 76. Over."

"Mohawk copies. Taking heavy machine gun and RPG fire from a six-man element inside compounds 65, 73, and 76. Break. Stand by for message to observer. Out."

"Apache 2-1 standing by for MTO. Over."

"Message to observer is as follows: section, gun one, three rounds HE (high explosive) in adjust, nine rounds HE fire for effect, target number AD1001. Out."

"Apache 2-1 copies gun one, three rounds HE in adjust, nine rounds HE fire for effect, target number AD1001. Over."

The first fire mission for 81s was going to me! I couldn't believe I finally had an opportunity to do it for real. It had only been two minutes, maybe less. We were still taking fire, answering with 5.56, 40mm, 7.62 from the M240B, and sniper shots from the M40. Mohawk had called back over net and said it would take a few seconds because of my request for danger close (anything under six hundred meters). They had to get approval from battalion for the mission and each adjustment I made. That was when I heard one of the best things in my life.

"Apache 2-1, mission approved for danger close. Time of flight 28 seconds. Shot. Over."

"Shot. Out."

"Splash. Over."

I was crossing my fingers. I was unsure how accurate the first round would be because it was the round they used to sink their base plate—or that's what he told me. I was not sure why they hadn't done it. It was already a danger close mission, and any amount of distance from the planned target had the potential to be dangerous.

I was scared as hell. I yelled to my boys, "Get down and cover up! Danger close with a wild one!"

We were in good hands. The first round impacted about two hundred meters to the left of the objective and about one hundred meters behind. Once that first round hit, the enemy fire slowed. At that point, I directed the snipers to move into a better position while the mortar rounds suppressed the enemy.

"Splash. Out. Adjust AD1001, drop one hundred fifty meters, right three hundred meters. Over."

"Roger. Drop one hundred fifty meters, right three hundred meters. Out."

At first, the adjustment was not approved. I wondered if something had gotten mixed up in the transmission from Mohawk to our battalion or if battalion was thinking something else. I had them send up the same adjustments again, and it was approved.

"Splash. Over."

As we waited for this round to impact, my machine gunner, Corporal Jefferson, moved his 240B into a better position. I will never forget what I saw. Corporal Jefferson went to pop his head over a small wall to get a good look, and an enemy 7.62 round impacted right in front of his face, breaking off the only piece of wall that was covering his head. He was fine though. Just a little shaken up. I later joked with him that he had almost died twice in three minutes.

"Splash. Out. Adjust AD1001, add five-zero, left one hundred. Over."

"Roger. Add five-zero, left one hundred. Out."

This round was my last adjustment, and everything was on at that point. As I was waiting for the final approval from Mohawk, we noticed a white van speeding off. It was difficult to get a good shot at it before it vanished.

"Splash. Over."

The round impacted right on the compound where the fire was coming from. Perfect shot!

"Splash. Out."

Then I got to say the three magic words. "Fire for effect!"

It was a pretty exciting moment for us since it was only the first day, and in the first few hours of moving, we were already engaged in a firefight and using 81mm mortars. The rounds impacted right on target, and the threat was completely eliminated, besides the van that got away.

Sergeant Pongo said he had seen three individuals wearing black inside the van but had quickly lost sight of it. I am not sure of the exact number, but when we searched the area of impact, we did not find any bodies. This became a trend since they were masters of cleaning up messes. The entire fire mission took about ten minutes. It was pretty quick despite having to wait for approval for each adjustment. I was pleased, but I thought Mohammed Gul knew more then he had told us. I thought, *This is going to be a long seven months!*

It was quiet after that for about ten minutes as we continued to move in the same direction. We were heading to a compound where we would link up as a platoon and go firm for about an hour. We picked up, got a head count, and made sure everybody was okay. It was hard to believe that nobody in my squad had been hit. It was as if there was a bulletproof bubble around us, and the rounds went everywhere but in it.

As we moved across the open field toward the next compound, my squad came under fire again. This time, it came from a compound to the northeast. While we were pushing up all morning, the enemy had set up a place that they were going to hold. The spot was just outside the small village known as Marjah Kalay. From our intelligence and other information, we expected it to be the place of attacks. Unfortunately, our route was directly in the center of this giant village, which was surrounded by little to nothing for cover.

We could see the impacts of their 7.62 AK-47 rounds hitting the ground all around, scattering shots and spitting up dirt but not hitting us. Everyone dropped to the deck and started to maneuver onto the compound.

I took the second fire team, and we ran about fifty meters under fire across the field slightly to the west of the compound as the rest of the squad provided cover fire. I felt as if I was playing Hot Potato except it was the ground that was hot. It was like walking on a hot beach; each time we stepped, we immediately brought our feet up. Every step was an awkward jump or skip, but we sprinted while screaming, "Shit. Shit. Shit. Shit. Shit. Shit. Shit. Shit!"

Corporal Bound's fire team posted up just north of the compound, and they were providing flank security as well as cover fire. As Bounds and I ran up to the entrance of the compound, I noticed a water well in front of us. I was so thirsty that—even under fire—I slid into the water pump like I was stealing home in the World Series. I slammed the pump several times to get a few drops of water to splash on my face and in my mouth.

Corporal Bounds yelled, "Sergeant Dyer, are you hit?"

"No!"

He had seen me drop so fast to pump the water that he thought I'd been hit and had fallen face-first. The shots suddenly stopped, and then they shifted fire to our flank fire teams to the east.

Bounds and I moved into the doorway to make entry, and Corporal Camacho's fire team was right behind us, ready to enter the compound. The doorway was heavily barricaded and blocked off with all kinds of obstacles around it. The thick metal door was attached securely to the mud hut walls; it was shut and locked. I did not expect to see an actual door as the main entrance to these compounds. Most of them were open and maybe had a curtain to cover the doorway.

I couldn't help but think this door was booby-trapped, I decided not to kick it in. I quickly turned to Corporal Bounds and had him pull out a stick of C-4.

I took out a prerigged blasting cap on a fifteen-second time delay fuse. I looked at him and said, "Today we test danger close."

We slapped the charge on the door and immediately took cover behind a tree. We were lying face down and praying we were far enough away. As we waited for the C-4 to detonate, I remembered being told about safety distances for training and safety standoff distances for combat. On that day, Bounds and I tested the new minimum safety distance!

Boom! My whole body rocked as wind, debris, and small pieces from the explosion flew by. We got up fast, and Camacho was right behind us with his fire team. It was very dusty, and my heart was beating intensely. I felt as if I had just sprinted four hundred meters, except I wasn't exhausted. I was excited and scared.

As we entered this compound, I had no idea what to expect. A few seconds earlier, we had been getting shot at from inside the compound, and now we were entering it with no element of surprise. Whoever was in there knew we were coming.

As we rounded the corner of what used to be the doorway, we saw a giant yard. It was nothing but dirt and was littered with bags of grain, trash, and a few chickens. Three Marines went right, and three went left with me. We quickly made our way to the doorway and scanned everything; years of close-quarters combat training ensured that we covered the entire environment.

In the midst of all the chaos, I got a call over the radio. Lieutenant Barhugesen asked if we had been hit by an IED.

I clicked the button and calmly said, "Nope. No IEDs here, just a stick of C-4 knocking."

Rocky said, "Attaboy!"

Female voices screamed, and children cried inside the compound.

Two of the Marines went around the building to inspect a white Toyota. The car had been backed in and hidden around the corner. It was close to the building, and the doors were barricaded. At first, I didn't know what to make of it—it seemed out of place—but as time went by, we learned that it was normal.

Camacho quickly checked the car, and nothing appeared suspicious.

I went inside the compound with Corporal Bounds, Corporal Rossol, Lance Corporal Miller, Lance Corporal Krupa, and my interpreter Ali, who we just called Jimmy. The compound had two floors, and the bottom floor was completely covered with bags of grain and hay. Stacks that were at least two to three bags high covered the whole bottom deck. We had to walk on top of the bags.

The door on the right was locked. A lot of screaming was coming from this room, and I was trying to get Jimmy to translate for me so I could figure out what was going on.

Two other Marines came up to a room with two males inside. They were yelling at the Marines, but nobody understood what they were saying. Another male was standing in the middle of the hallway with his hands at his side. He appeared to be in his thirties, was very calm, and acted the opposite of everyone else. He was just staring at us. Perhaps he was in shock. An hour earlier, he might have been making love to his wife, and then these weird-looking Americans wearing tons of gear, pissed, tired, hungry, and dirty blew up his door and rushed into his home. He could have been waiting for us the whole time, planning and coordinating the multiple ambushes we were encountering. All of this came within seconds of entering the house.

We had been searching houses all morning and talking with Afghans, but this one seemed almost impossible. There was so much going on at that point that it was difficult to find a place to start. I had security posted up outside the house. I had one fire team with me, and another fire team with snipers was still outside, engaging the enemy from the east.

Sergeant Pongo's snipers were able to eliminate the threat without any injuries on our part. I decided to keep two Marines downstairs to keep an eye on the three men. I took the rest of my team and searched the rest of the house. We came up with no real threats, and we went back to question the residents individually. The questions were simple and basic. Even though we had been shot at all morning from all different angles—and even from this guy's house—he was evasive when I asked him if he knew anything about it.

"No. I have not heard anything all day. It has been really quiet. Maybe some tractors working in the fields. I was outside working in my garden when you blew up my door, and my family is scared, hiding inside."

Using my terp, I asked if he heard the bombs going off, referring to the nine 81mm mortar rounds I had used to blow up the neighboring compound. It was not exactly a quiet explosion, and I had even taken out his neighbor's house!

"No. No, sir. I don't know what you are talking about. I didn't hear anything, and I don't know who was shooting at you."

It was frustrating because that was the story all day long. Nobody saw anything, and nobody knew anything. Even though I had fourteen Marines behind me that could attest that the shots came from his compound and the adjacent one, we had nothing to prove it. We had no weapons and no brass of any type.

I decided to pick up and continue on our path to link up. If we stayed, we would have kept playing the question game, and I was already tired of this circle of questions and dealing with those people.

We moved out of the building with all our limbs attached and continued on to our link up spot, which was about a hundred yards away.

I got a call on the radio from 1 Actual (our platoon commander), and he said our squad was covered and had security. There was a tree line that basically led directly to it.

I put the snipers in the middle of our formation, and we moved in a very direct manner because the remainder of the platoon was set up to provide watch and security for us.

We were not even thirty seconds outside of the compound when more shots rang out. This time, they came from two different directions, to our left and directly behind us. Although the platoon had security, it was difficult to see everything. What a shitty situation to be in. We learned quickly that no matter which route we took, no matter how much dispersion we had, or how much cover/concealment we thought we had, there was always an opening for them to shoot at us.

As I hit the deck, I looked over and saw the snipers on the ground. For some reason, they were not firing. I yelled, "Corporal Pongo, do you have eyes on?"

He yelled, "Yes, but there is no way in hell I am dropping this watermelon!"

Outside the last compound, Corporal Pongo had picked up a watermelon and was carrying it like a football in his left arm. He held his rifle in his right arm. His main dilemma was whether to drop the watermelon or hold on to it. It was so incredibly hot, and the taste of that watermelon seemed worth the risk. When he dove to the ground in the prone position, he looked like a football player who refused to drop the ball. I am not making light of combat, but I think that only someone in that situation would appreciate the humor of the moment.

I sent Corporal Camacho's fire team to run directly to the link up building while everyone provided cover fire.

Corporal Pongo started unleashing his M40, taking out at least three guys from three hundred to four hundred yards away—while holding on to his damn watermelon.

Someone yelled, "Oh my god. Did you see that gut shot?"

Corporal Pongo was a skilled shooter. I fired back at what I thought were four guys in prone positions about two hundred yards to my left.

Lance Corporal McHugh's fire team took rear security. Since we were in an open field, I didn't want to stay there any longer. I made the call to run by fire team to our link up. As one team picked up and moved, another team provided cover fire so that the enemy was suppressed and could not fire back.

Corporal Pongo and I were the last ones to get up, ensuring the Marines made it safely. We picked up and ran like crazy into cover. I thought I was a fast runner until that day when I was trying to outrun bullets. I may have just gotten lucky—or maybe I really was a fast runner.

Corporal Pongo and I made it to friendly lines, and for the first time since being dropped off, the whole platoon was in one place. We saw all the squad leaders, the platoon sergeant, the platoon commander, and the fire team of British Marines we had attached to the platoon as guides. The other Marines were providing security on the outside, and they had every avenue of approach covered by fire and observation.

The platoon was tactically proficient, and every Marine knew his job and the job of the person above him. The compound was secure. Corporal Pongo had his guys in place to reach out beyond what our guys could. Although we were right in the middle of an abandoned compound and in the open, we were relying on tactics used since the beginning of the Marine Corps to protect us—360-degree security, automatic weapons covering the most likely areas of approach, and all avenues of approach covered by fire and/or observation.

I walked around the compound while the platoon went firm in order to conduct a short tactical pause. This would give us some time to rest, regroup, refit, reorganize, and prepare ourselves for the next movement. It was the first time I had seen the other squads since Camp Leatherneck. We had all left in different sticks, and when we landed, each squad had its own sector of responsibility. Although our movements from insert point up to that point were basically online with one another, we hadn't been together for what felt like days.

The Marines looked exhausted. That thousand-yard stare people always talk about appeared on everyone's faces. Eyes were a little darker, perhaps because everyone was tired and dehydrated. Beards looked like they had been growing for days. Uniforms were ripped, dirty, and drenched in sweat. Boots were unbloused, and sleeves were rolled up to forearms. Kneepads that had once started firmly around the knees were now around ankles. The only way to feel somewhat normal was by developing new fashion statements. They had smiles on their face, and were just happy to see one another. Besides those providing security, most of them fell asleep against the wall. I am sure their bodies had been drained of all energy, and pure adrenaline had kept them up. Once that adrenaline wore off, the body crashed—and it crashed hard. There was nothing to keep you awake once your body decides it has reached its apex and wants to shut down. Severe fatigue—what I call battle fatigue—set in.

MCDP1-3 tactics states, "Along with the tangible assets used as a reserve, the prudent commander must also be aware of, and plan for, the intangible factors that impact on combat power and its sustainment." One of those intangible factors is fatigue, which we knew would happen. Many books about combat note that one cannot sustain constant combat for long periods of time without losing train of thought or taking a break. This was clearly the case.

Some of Corporal Hoard's Marines were relaxing in the abandoned, dilapidated mud brick compound. Lance Corporal Michuad, Lance Corporal Gentry, and Lance Corporal Hogan's dusty-brown uniforms were stained with perspiration, and they were passed out while still sitting up. Lance Corporal Shannon and Staff Sergeant Collins were fighting to keep their eyes open. A few were exchanging war stories of what they had encountered. A few were laughing, but mostly there were stoic conversations and amazement that we were all still alive and had not suffered any casualties.

I walked into the inner compound, and one of the Marines behind a M249 SAW said, "Sergeant Dyer, they are straight ahead. Semper Fi!"

"Thanks, brotha," I said and walked into the part of the house where they were. The room was small, around ten by fifteen feet, and it seemed to fit everyone okay. I saw the squad leaders (Rocky and Pancho), the platoon's dog handler (Sergeant Elizondo), our platoon sergeant (Staff Sergeant O'Brian), the platoon commander (Second Lieutenant Barghusen), his radio operator (Lance Corporal Espinol), two British Marines, and our news photographer (Lucian Read).

I felt a giant sense of relief when I walked into that room. I called over the radio and told all three teams to conduct a full gear check and to redistribute ammo and water as needed. As soon as I got the confirmation that my team leaders were up on all gear, I put down my M-4 and threw off my pack, jacket with SAPI plates, a million attachments, and my Kevlar helmet. I was drenched in sweat, exhausted, tired, hungry, and thirsty, but I felt so relieved to have that gear off of my body.

I looked over my gear and realized I had lost my Garmin GPS. *Shit! You've got to be kidding me!* I looked over all my gear twice but found nothing. Who knows where it could have fallen, and the kicker was I had everything tied down—or "dummy corded"—to my gear. This was the *one* piece of gear I didn't because it fit snug into my pouch. I was more concerned with how the Company XO would respond. He was a prick. Nobody liked him, and he was a challenge to work with. I could see it now—busted down in rank, kicked out of the company, and sent home early because I lost a $150 GPS in a firefight! Just my luck.

We all came together in a little circle like a football team during a huddle. We broke out our maps and conducted a short debrief, basically going over our 5 Ws (who, what, when, where, and why) of the past several hours and we confirmed and denied parts of the intelligence we had gathered prior to insertion. We put down all the places each squad had taken contact and started to collectively build an idea of what was going on.

The firefights from larger compounds had happened within two clicks (two grid squares or approximately two thousand meters). It appeared that the enemy was moving north, setting up ambushes, bounding to the north, and repeating. This made perfect sense and proved what we all were thinking. We went over our routes and each squad's mission again to ensure that we all knew the plan.

After the platoon commander repeated a few key points, we gathered up our gear, strapped back up, buttoned our chin straps, and moved out. My squad was the first to move out of the compound. We pushed slightly northeast, and then we were going to head north. The next objective was to make it about two more clicks to where the British had mapped out a possible area to rest for the night. On the way, we were going to check out two company objectives. The third objective was a suspected Taliban hangout; we were also going to pay a visit to a known Taliban fighter's house. His name was Agha Sayed.

My squad exited the compound and moved out into an open field. The open fields were hard to avoid in any direction. Part of our workup training was patrolling in open danger areas. We could only use the tree lines to mask our movement occasionally. If we wanted to get to our objectives, we had to patrol through the open. It was extremely nerve-racking to know the enemy could see us before we saw them. All they had to do was pop around any one of the million corners of a compound, fire a burst of 7.62, and run back inside. This made for a joyous time, moving from one position to another position. It was never a matter of *if* we would get shot at; it was always a matter of *when* we would get shot at.

An adjacent compound was separated by a tree line between us and Route Keystone, which we needed to get to in order to get to our next objective. We crossed the tree line and set up security on the outside of the compound, covering all the avenues of approach.

I brought my terp and Camacho's fire team into the compound to talk to anyone who lived there. I made every effort to talk to anybody I could while we searched the compound. Most of the locals I interacted with didn't mind and would say it was okay to look around. Even if they were hiding something inside, they would lie and tell me that it isn't theirs—or they had no idea how it got there—once we found it. It happened so many times.

Two males were standing there. They looked scared and stayed close to the walls. I asked them their names and ran them down the list of names we had of individuals of interest. I also asked if anyone else lived there. While I was talking with them, Camacho's fire team searched the compound. The names didn't match with anything we had, but I took the basic info to help build our AO board: names, ages, occupations, how long they had lived there, compound number in reference to our GRG, and an eight-digit grid. I did this for every single compound we went to.

After ten minutes, Camacho sent over the radio that they didn't see anything unusual. The two individuals told me they lived there with their family, and the rest of them were in another room. The gunshots and explosions had scared them, and everyone hid. I looked around for a few more minutes and decided it was a waste of time. Another compound, another bust; somebody had weapons around there, and somebody had to know who was shooting at us.

I walked out of the compound and radioed to the outside security. I told them to break down and told the team leaders to push out toward our next objective. At that point, the Marines were exhausted. I could see it in their eyes, their body language, and their movements. What started out as taking a knee on security halts transitioned into taking a prone position after five minutes. Then it went directly to sitting against a tree or other type of support.

The movement up to objective three was pretty quiet. There weren't too many local nationals walking around; we saw a few motorbikes on the road and a few farmers tending their crops, the normal sights and sounds of Nawa.

The limit of advance for us was not to pass our right lateral limit, which was Route Shiner, and the area we wanted to go was just south of Route Natty Rock. There was a little village with about twenty compounds.

We made our way closer to what we suspected was Agha Sayed's home, and I stopped just short of the building. We were about two hundred meters short of our objective, and I held everyone up. There were a group of kids a hundred meters to the north. I raised my rifle and looked through my scope to get a better look.

The four kids and an adult had a radio or a cell phone. It was hard to make out from a distance, but I could see a solid dark-colored object and an antenna. My heart started to pound because I had no idea what it could be. Several thoughts came to mind, but I treated it as a possible spotter for the Taliban who was radioing our position, number of Marines, and direction of movement to them.

I called over to Sergeant Pongo on the squad net to see if he could see something I couldn't. He confirmed what I'd seen and told me he had a clean shot if I wanted him to take it. I smiled and told him to wait it out. The last thing I wanted to be responsible for was shooting a kid.

I grabbed Bounds and his team, and we moved up and to the east to get a better view. We moved to a building that was directly alongside Shiner. I took cover behind a corner. I grabbed my camera to capture a huge marijuana bush that was taller than I was—and perhaps four times as wide. As soon as I took it out, a burst of AK-47 shots rang out. Crack. Crack. Crack. Crack. Crack.

I immediately dropped to a knee and looked around to see if I could see anything. I called over the radio to see if anyone had a visual or any idea where the shots had come from.

Sergeant Elizondo was right next me. He laughed and said, "Dyer, every time you take your camera out, someone shoots at us. I think they are on to you."

I thought about it for a second, and he was actually correct.

Pongo called over the radio and said, "Dyer, those kids are on the move. They are running away, heading into the compound directly to their west."

I got the squad up, and we moved quickly toward the compound. It was isolated, alone, and had a little stream running along the exterior wall. A wall separated the compound from the opening to the field, and the only entrance was across a little footbridge, which the kids had run across.

Stoner took the CMD (which is our IED sweeper, like a metal detector) and scanned the footbridge for IEDs.

We proceeded across, walked into the compound area, and asked if anyone was home. No sound. We looked into the actual rooms, but nobody was there. The kids had either snuck out the back or were hiding somewhere. I didn't want to waste any time because it was already late, and we still had some objectives ahead of us.

We moved toward Agha Sayed's compound, paralleling Shiner and utilizing the road and the open field. Although the roads were never safe places to walk, it allowed us to move a little quicker and utilize Hitch, our IED-sniffing black Lab.

I patrolled beside Elizondo and Hitch. Elizondo would call out commands, and Hitch would obey each and every one. They had a good working relationship, and if anyone should be in the most dangerous spot, it should be me as the squad leader.

As we approached the compound, we noticed that it was definitely bigger than a majority of the ones we had seen and searched. It had a big outer wall, like most, but it also had multiple little footbridges and several cars parked inside. It had an upstairs and a huge garden on the inside. It was very well kept.

We made our way in and were approached by a clean-looking older gentleman. He didn't have dirty clothes, and his hands didn't appear to be dirty. I thought I had hit the jackpot; this was our man. I asked for his name and explained why we were there.

His name was Hafez Allah, and he claimed to be a village doctor. The Taliban had closed his facility, and he was scared to reopen it.

I asked if he knew Agha Sayed. He claimed to never have heard of him. "Maybe he lives on the other side of town." Hafez Allah pointed southwest toward Marjah Kalay.

I was about to ask if anyone else lived there when one of my Marines yelled out that he had two adult males walking toward him from around the corner.

We walked over, stopped them, searched them, and started to talk with them. Nobody knew Agha Sayed, and they said their names were Aziz Ahmad and Abdul Resheed.

Bounds' fire team searched the compound while I talked with the three men. None of them had heard of Agha Sayed, but they did tell us that the person we should be going after was a Taliban commander named Haji Nafas Khan. Khan was a bad guy with twenty or twenty-five people working underneath him. We knew Khan was the ANP commander, but the three men agreed that he was a Taliban commander. I felt like I had just unlocked groundbreaking news that could change the whole deployment.

I pictured the headlines: *US Marine takes down ANP commander as he connects link to Taliban.*

I radioed the information to our platoon commander and told him I would continue to search the area for more information. As far as we all knew, this was Agha Sayed's building, and any of the three guys could have been him.

After thirty minutes of talking and searching, I checked in with Bounds. The place had a lot of equipment and supplies that led him to believe it had been a clinic at some point. If not, they were addicted to heroin and had a lot of needles. I supposed both were possible in that area.

I decided to pull out. It was getting late, and we had a link up point to establish and possibly rest there for the night. I called over the net that 2-1 was heading to the link up position, and we continued to push north.

The link up position was a compound that the Brits and the ANA had mapped out, and I believe they paid the owner of the compound to let us stay for the night. They also compensated them for their watermelons since there were quite a few growing around it. They knew we were going to enjoy them!

It had been a long day, and we had only completed a portion of the distance that we needed to cover. The tactical pause for the night was much needed.

As night came near and the sun went down, I walked into the courtyard. Marines were talking and sharing stories. Lance Corporal Hogan was sitting on the ground and using his pack as a backrest. His hands were on his head while he reflected on the previous twenty-four hours. Like most of us, he was probably wondering what the hell had just happened.

Lance Corporal Lemus was staring at the ground next to Hogan, perhaps thinking about the same thing. The looks on their faces said it all. They were warriors—nineteen, twenty, twenty-one—fighting in a country they had never been to for a purpose they couldn't quite grasp. For the next seven months, this would be their duty—every second, every hour, and every day. This was a realistic snapshot of what was to come.

I looked at them and smiled. I was proud to be a part of that organization and knew it was all in a day's work.

Summary of Action

Action Dates: 07/02/2009–07/03/2009
Unit (At Time of Action) 1STBN 5THMAR 1STMARDIV
Geographical Location: Helmand Province, Afghanistan, Nawa
Operation: Operation Enduring Freedom (Khanjar)

Summary of Action:

Each individual included on this recommendation has been screened and has not previously received the Combat Action Ribbon for Operation Enduring Freedom.

On 02 July 2009, in Nawa district, Helmand Province, Afghanistan, first squad, second platoon, company A, First Battalion, 5th Marines made contact with enemy fighters during three separate engagements. The first engagement occurred at 1100 with small arms enemy fire composed of AK-47s, RPKs, and RPGs, approximately 400 meters to our east from a 6 to 8 man team. The whole squad immediately took cover as all fire teams returned fire with 203-40mm grenades, M4-5.56, M40-7.62, and M240B machine gun (MG)-7.62. First fire team established a base of fire, second fire team ranged distances and fired a Light Armored Weapon (LAW) as we took (1) RPG round above us, and third fire team provided rear security. MGs fired for 20 seconds at the rapid rate, then approximately 60 seconds at the sustained. Sgt Dyer called in Mohawk (81s) in order to (IOT) get indirect fires (IDF) to allow first squad to maneuver. The fire mission was danger close (under 600 meters) and was approved. Once the first IDF round impacted, snipers maneuvered 30 meters east to a better vantage point which allowed them to shoot independently on (3) suspected MG positions. As the IDF rounds hit, the enemy fires ceased and the reaming enemy ran to a white van and sped away south west. No injuries occurred.

The second engagement occurred at 1230 with small arms enemy fire composed of AK-47s and RPKs from the northeast, approximately 200 meters from a 3 to 5 man team. Immediately first fire team and snipers laid down a base of fire while third fire team provided rear security. Sgt Dyer, along with second fire team, moved under fire to the compound and breeched the secured hatch with C-4 on a fifteen-second time fuse. We then made entry and cleared the building but all enemy had fled out the back to the northeast. The remaining squad then moved into the compound to reorganize. The enemy fires quickly stopped and the situation died down. First squad went firm, put up security, and awaited the location to do a platoon link up. No injuries occurred.

The third engagement occurred at 1400 with small arms enemy fire composed of AK-47s and RPKs from the west, approximately 300 meters from a 3 to 5 man team. Sgt Dyer and Sgt Pongo laid down a base of fire while the remainder of the squad bounded to the platoon link up position (Bldg #12 J3J) to get some cover and concealment. Once they were in place and suppression fires from the platoon started, Sgt Dyer and Sgt Pongo moved into cover and concealment to join the rest of the platoon. Snipers then set in with second fire team and suppressed the enemy until fires ceased. No injuries occurred.

Sgt Lucas A. Dyer as the Squad Leader returned fire with (10) 5.56 rounds at enemy forces in a compound, 6 to 8 man size, 400 meters east of his position. SNM directed first fire team to establish a base of fire while second fire team ranged distances to prep a Light Armored Weapon (LAW) and 203-40mm rounds, and ordered third fire team to provide rear security, as well as for Cpl Jefferson to get to a better position to get the M240B machine gun firing. Enemy fires increased and rounds impacted within inches, which had the squad pinned down and unable to maneuver. SNM then called into Mohawk (81s) IOT get indirect fires on the enemy position. The fire mission was approved for danger close. Once IDF rounds impacted enemy fires slowed and SNM directed snipers to maneuver to a better position to fire independently on what they suspected as (3) possible machine gun positions. SNMs fire mission dropped (9) HE 81mm rounds. During the second engagement, Sgt Dyer returned fire with (3) 5.56 rounds at enemy forces in a compound, 3 to 5 man size, 200 meters northeast of his position. SNM directed first fire team to establish a base of fire along with snipers and machine guns, and for third fire team to provide rear security IOT allow SNM and second fire team to maneuver to the compound. While under enemy fire, SNM, along with second fire team, maneuvered to the compound and breached the barricaded hatch with a stick of C-4 on a fifteen-second time delay fuse. Once inside, SNM and second fire team searched and cleared the compound. The enemy fire ceased. SNM and second fire team secured the compound and provided security while the remainder of the squad moved in. During the third engagement, Sgt Dyer returned fire with (20) 5.56 rounds at the enemy forces in a tree line 300 meters west of his position. SNM laid down a base of fire IOT allow the remaining squad to move into the platoon link up position for cover and concealment.

Cpl Manuel E. Camacho, the first team leader, returned fire with (6) 5.56 rounds and (2) 40mm rounds at enemy forces in a compound 400 meters east of his position. SNM issued additional ADDRACs for his fire team and gave directions and distances as enemy forces moved in and out of the compound. During the second engagement, Cpl Camacho returned fire with (1) 5.56 rounds and (2) 40mm rounds at enemy forces in a compound 200 meters northeast of his position. SNM issued additional ADDRACs for his fire team and gave directions and distances as enemy forces moved in and out of the compound.

LCpl Paul J. Stoner, as first fire team rifleman, returned fire with (10) 5.56 rounds at enemy forces in a compound 400 meters east of his position. During the second engagement, LCpl Stoner returned fire at enemy forces in a compound 200 meters northeast of his position.

LCpl Alberto B. Hernandez, as first fire team saw gunner, returned fire with (25) 5.56 link at enemy forces in a compound 400 meters east of his position. SNM opened up with a 10 round burst, and then fired several 3 to 4 round bursts over the next several minutes. During the second engagement, LCpl Hernandez returned fire at enemy forces in a compound 200 meters northeast of his position.

Cpl John A. Bounds, as second fire team leader, returned fire with
(4) 40mm rounds and (1) LAW at enemy forces in a compound
400 meters east of his position. SNM, under fire prepped, ranged
distance, and fired the LAW, causing the enemy fire to slow. SNM
then used his M203 to fire (4) 40mm rounds to keep the enemy
suppressed. SNM also issued additional ADDRACs and gave
direction and distances to his fire team as enemy forces moved
in and out of the compound. During the second engagement,
Cpl Bounds returned fire at enemy forces in a compound 200
meters northeast of his position. While under enemy fire SNM,
maneuvered to the compound and provided security while
the barricaded hatch was blown by Sgt Dyer with a stick of
C-4 on a fifteen-second time delay fuse. Once inside, SNM
searched and cleared the compound with his fire team. SNM
then provided security to allow the rest of the squad to move
inside. During the third engagement, Cpl Bounds returned fire
at enemy forces in a tree line 300 meters west of his position.

Cpl Jordy D. Rossol, as second fire team rifleman, returned
fire at enemy forces in a compound 400 meters east of his
position. During the second engagement, Cpl Rossol returned
fire at enemy forces in a compound 200 meters northeast of
his position. While under enemy fire, SNM maneuvered to
the compound and provided security while the barricaded
hatch was blown by Sgt Dyer with a stick of C-4 on a fifteen-
second time delay fuse. Once inside, SNM searched and
cleared the compound with his fire team. SNM then provided
security to allow the rest of the squad to move inside.

LCpl John M. Krupa, as second fire team saw gunner, returned
fire at enemy forces in a compound 400 meters east of his

LUCAS A. DYER

position. SNM gave the original ADDRAC and helped direct fire onto the enemy position. SNM also assisted Sgt Dyer in spotting the impacts of the fire mission IOT help get rounds on target. During the second engagement, LCpl Krupa returned fire at enemy forces in a compound 200 meters northeast of his position. While under enemy fire, SNM maneuvered to the compound and provided security while the barricaded hatch was blown by Sgt Dyer with a stick of C-4 on a fifteen-second time delay fuse. Once inside, SNM searched and cleared the compound with his fire team. SNM then provided security to allow the rest of the squad to move inside.

LCpl Jamie D. Miller, as second fire team Designated Marksmen (DM), returned fire at enemy forces in a compound 400 meters east of his position. During the second engagement, LCpl Miller returned fire at enemy forces in a compound 200 meters northeast of his position. While under enemy fire, SNM maneuvered to the compound and provided security while the barricaded hatch was blown by Sgt Dyer with a stick of C-4 on a fifteen-second time delay fuse. Once inside, SNM searched and cleared the compound with his fire team. SNM then provided security to allow the rest of the squad to move inside.

Cpl Brandon C. Ladner, as second fire team rifleman, attached to first squad, returned fire at enemy forces in a compound 400 meters east of his position. During the second engagement, Cpl Ladner returned fire at enemy forces in a compound 200 meters northeast of his position. While under enemy fire, SNM maneuvered to the compound and provided security while the barricaded hatch was blown by Sgt Dyer with a stick of C-4 on a fifteen-second time delay fuse. Once inside, SNM searched and cleared the compound with his fire team. SNM then provided security to allow the rest of the squad to move inside. During the third engagement Cpl Ladner returned fire at enemy forces in a tree line 300 meters west of his position.

LCpl Robert L. McHugh, as third fire team leader, returned fire at enemy forces in a compound 400 meters east of his position. SNM also coordinated rear security with his fire team covering the squads rear with at least two Marines at all times. During the second engagement, LCpl McHugh returned fire at enemy forces in a compound 200 meters northeast of his position. SNM also coordinated rear security with his fire team covering the squads rear with at least two Marines at all times. During the third engagement, LCpl McHugh returned fire at enemy forces in a tree line 300 meters west of his position.

LCpl Ducan H. Mai, as third fire team rifleman, returned fire at enemy forces in a compound 400 meters east of his position. SNM also coordinated rear security with his fire team covering the squads rear with at least two Marines at all times. During the second engagement, LCpl Mai returned fire at enemy forces in a compound 200 meters northeast of his position. SNM also coordinated rear security with his fire team covering the squads rear with at least two Marines at all times. During the third engagement, LCpl Mai returned fire at enemy forces in a tree line 300 meters west of his position.

LCpl Antonio Martinez, as third fire team saw gunner, returned fire at enemy forces in a compound 400 meters east of his position. SNM also coordinated rear security with his fire team covering the squads rear with at least two Marines at all times.

During the second engagement, LCpl Martinez returned fire at enemy forces in a compound 200 meters northeast of his position. SNM also coordinated rear security with his fire team covering the squads rear with at least two Marines at all times. During the third engagement, LCpl Martinez returned fire at enemy forces in a tree line 300 meters west of his position.

Cpl Madison J. Jefferson, as a machine gun squad leader attached to first squad, returned fire at enemy forces in a compound 400 meters east of his position. SNM controlled the rates of fire and gave the ADDRAC for the M240B. During the second engagement, Cpl Jefferson returned fire at enemy forces in a compound 200 meters northeast of his position. SNM controlled all fires for the M240B and gave all ADDRACs.

LCpl Jamil D. Allen, as a machine gunner attached to first squad, returned fire at enemy forces in a compound 400 meters east of his position. During the second engagement, LCpl Allen returned fire at enemy forces in a compound 200 meters northeast of his position. During the third engagement, LCpl Allen returned fire at enemy forces in a tree line 300 meters west of his position.

HM3 Nicholos A. Beck, as the corpsman for first squad, returned fire at enemy forces in a compound 400 meters east of his position. During the second engagement, HM3 Beck returned fire at enemy forces in a compound 200 meters northeast of his position.

Sgt Diego D. Pongo, as the sniper team leader attached to first squad, returned fire at enemy forces in a compound 400 meters east of his position. As the enemy fires slowed, SNM took his team and maneuvered 30 meters east to a tree line IOT fire on what SNM suspected to be (3) machine gun positions. SNM assisted in helping the squad identify enemy forces using his spotter. During the second engagement, Sgt Pongo returned fire at enemy forces in a compound 200 meters northeast of his position. During the third engagement, Sgt Pongo returned fire at the enemy forces in a tree line 300 meters west of his position. SNM laid down a base of fire IOT allow the remaining squad to move into the platoon link up position for cover and concealment.

LCpl Dexter Hegerhorst, as a sniper attached to first squad, returned fire at enemy forces in a compound 400 meters east of his position. As the enemy fires slowed, SNM maneuvered 30 meters east to a tree line IOT fire on what SNM suspected to be (3) machine gun positions. During the second engagement, LCpl Dexter returned fire at enemy forces in a compound 200 meters northeast of his position.

LCpl Nicholas Green, as a sniper attached to first squad, returned fire at enemy forces in a compound 400 meters east of his position. As the enemy fires slowed, SNM maneuvered 30 meters east to a tree line IOT fire on what SNM suspected to be (3) machine gun positions. During the second engagement, LCpl Green returned fire at enemy forces in a compound 200 meters northeast of his position.

CHAPTER IV

GAINING TRUST FROM THE PEOPLE TAKES MORE THAN A WEAPON

Know your patch! Know the people, the topography, economy, history, and culture. Know every village, road, field, population group, tribal leader, and ancient grievance. Your task is to become the world expert on your particular district ... Neglect this knowledge, and it will kill you.
—Dr. David Kilcullen

Our area of operation (AO) was developed around the *population first* strategy rather than *enemy first*. In other words, we focused on the people of Nawa first, and then we would worry about the enemy. I told my Marines over and over that it didn't matter if they liked the people or not. I didn't really care if they thought the ideology was bullshit. If we wanted to win, the people had to believe that we were sincere—and we had to convince them that it was in their best interests to support us.

Winning was what mattered, and the only way to do that was to get better at counterinsurgency operations, regardless of how much we hated it. The general vision for our AO was to create a zone of security, economic activity, and increased freedom of movement for the majority of the region's most populated areas.

By clearing and securing the areas influenced by the Taliban, we would conceivably enable a zone of stability throughout our AO. The scale of this challenge would be matched by the resources we had. In order to do this, several changes were made to our tactical level of fighting and planning as a company and at the small unit leader level.

Our company made developmental, governance, information operations, and partnering with Afghanistan National Security Forces (ANSF) our primary means of operations. The focus was on the people of Helmand, local nationals, and villages. This strategy focused on empowering local leaders—specifically village elders—providing protection for the local population, mentoring, and improving local infrastructure. Our constant focus on the population's well-being helped isolate the insurgency, making operations more defined and resulting in less collateral damage. As this process continued, we slowly gained the cooperation and support of local leaders. In time, we found that employing this method—and utilizing it as the primary fighting tool—created the most logical and successful conditions for counterinsurgency (COIN) operations.

In order for us to be successful at counterinsurgency, it is critical to have an in-depth understanding of COIN, what COIN involves, requires, and most importantly, what the people need, not want. That simple method of giving the people what they needed—not what they wanted—was logical and dependable. I even used it with my Marines. Everyone would thank us for it later.

While keeping all of that in mind, it was just as important to keep the ever-changing and ever-adapting enemy from defeating anyone weaker than our force, and keeping the local populace away from the insurgency. We had to understand COIN, how to operate at the small unit level (tactical), and how to execute the intent from a higher level (strategic).

Knowing COIN and being able to execute what we knew were two different things that needed to become synonymous. When referring to what the people needed versus what they wanted, I believe there was a difference. For example, incorporating the ANSF was something they needed—but understandably might not have wanted at first.

Making developmental operations based on what they needed was a great way to produce short-term and long-term solutions. It had to be done and would take time. We couldn't walk right in and expect to make changes. We knew that the three block war theory was always being tested and as you found yourself on one block shaking hands and taking notes, you would walk into the next block of tracking down and hunting the enemy in order to kill him. Then with no break in between you would be turning back around to those very people you were shaking hands with, helping them out with humanitarian assistance.

In most cases, I believe that the enemy needs to be killed. The enemy lives among the population, which makes it hard to distinguish between friend and foe. So how do you do it? How do you figure out who the enemy is? How do you know the difference between the insurgency or the anti-ANSF, anticoalition forces and the locals who were on the fence, holding neutral positions? How can you tell the difference between a family feud and an actual hostile act? You do this by knowing your patch. You do this by knowing the people—elders and kids—and by living with them. You are doing more than just patrolling into a village and conducting meet and greets. You are with them every day, doing all you can to become an expert in your particular village.

The term *presence patrol* should not be in the tactical vocabulary. It does nothing as a long-term solution to just show up without a purpose or intent. If your intent is to only talk to a few local nationals, you have already set yourself up to fail. You should not set a number or a standard for how many you interact with. It should be *always*. Mere presence alone does not equal mission accomplishment, and counterinsurgency will fail without a stable government.

When referring to the tactical level, I am talking about the lowest level of war. In military doctrine, tactics refer to the concepts and methods used to accomplish a particular mission in combat or other military operations. In our sense, it is used and practiced at the squad leader level and down. Small unit leaders are the key to success of counterinsurgency operations, specifically in this case, since they are applying the application of combat power on the battlefield in order to defeat the enemy.

The small unit leaders are winning engagements and battles. They combine firepower and maneuvers to achieve success in combat, just as they combine tactical patience to achieve success in noncombat operations. Most small unit leaders have an understanding and grasp the concept of incorporating tactics, techniques, and procedures (TTPs). Tactics require quick decisions that are mastered through realistic training and repetition. Tactics are *the* way to accomplish any mission; techniques are *a* way, leaving procedures as a combination of both.

It is safe to say that in most combat environments—whether you are using COIN or not—TTPs can be used in place of standard operating procedures (SOPs), if done correctly. Tactics are the way to accomplish missions, and they are equally useful when applying standard methods.

SOPs are good, and they are used everywhere, but I feel that they limit you when executing. In combat, you have to be flexible, and you have to adapt, sometimes on the go, leaving your plan to more of a calculated action based on circumstance. If you combine procedures using tactics and techniques, you have several options available. You have the way, and then you have several other options to accomplish the same mission by utilizing techniques. This is more for planning purposes, but they will help you execute with more reliability.

The strategic level of war is the highest level of war. Activities at the strategic level of war focus directly on policy objectives. Although not generated by the small unit leaders, the small unit leaders have a tremendous impact on the successes and failures at that level. The *strategic corporal*—a phrase coined by US Marine General Charles Krulak, thirty-first commandant of the Marine Corps—is a great example of this.

Small unit leaders on the ground constantly make decisions and choices that affect the current operations and follow units up to the political spectrum. In this context, it will be referred to as a way of winning wars and securing peace. In order to do so, we had to have goals, objectives, and solid plans that included the use of combined assists including ANSF. We understood that the short-term solution was not going to create a safer Afghanistan or allow security, peace, and prosperity to be restored. The long-term goal would achieve that. Small unit leaders had to understand what the objective was at our level, and more importantly, how our level in upcoming months would allow the incoming units to be just as successful. I am very confident that we accomplished that.

Considering this, and taking both short-term and long-term goals into perspective, I was able to link the strategic and tactical levels together. I was able to use the tactical results to attain strategic objectives. MCDP 1 states, "This level includes deciding when, where, and under what conditions to engage the enemy in battle—and when, where, and under what conditions to refuse battle in support of higher aims."

When you have the idea or plan in place to win a battle, you must apply that idea or plan by utilizing tactics. You must have a means of winning and a final result desired to achieve these results. They go hand in hand, leaving the operational level as the final step in acting. I believe that these three levels are similar to a three-legged stool. The stool has its strong base when all three legs are touching the floor. If you take away a leg, the stool becomes unstable. It becomes unstable to the point where the base is no longer strong, and the three-legged stool will fall, ultimately failing at its purpose.

If you have a means to win, but no way to achieve the objective, ultimately you will fail at your strategic objectives. The objective operationally was more than driving out the Taliban of the areas they controlled; we had to secure the area to allow the Afghan government to operate. The short-term goal was aimed to improve security ahead of presidential elections for August 20, 2009, which would allow voter registration for the first time in the Helmand Province. The long-term goal was to help restore security, peace, and prosperity, eventually allowing Afghanistan's local government agencies to take over security.

A counterinsurgency operation in full spectrum is hard to get used to. You have to be a people person in order to succeed, and as mentioned, you must believe in what you are fighting for. In most cases, we won this battle without using our firepower. It really does take more than a weapon. It took months to get to the point that Alpha Company was when we changed over with Charlie Company First Battalion, Third Marines.

The people of Afghanistan wanted us there and needed our security. We made it mandatory to treat them with respect as if they were family. This mentality was universal within the company, and it really went without saying. In doing this, the people of Afghanistan opened up their villages to us. They invited us in for food and chai (tea), and they told us what we needed to know as long as we kept their trust. We worked hard to get the village elders and the local population on our side, and then the Mullah, and then anyone else we could think of. For the first time in decades, they had an elected government. We used their elected officials as a great source to help us sort out issues.

In our AO, each village or group of villages was represented by someone. I found it a good rule when interacting with local nationals to mimic their culture when possible. I attempted to learn as much Pashto as I could and tried to speak the native language. I found it very helpful to know how to start every conversation and end every conversation while understanding key words in between. I would have my interpreter do the rest.

They loved to talk, and more importantly, they tended to complain about what they didn't like. I got a lot of good information from twenty-minute conversations, and I was always prepared for a gathering of local nationals. I would have something short—but important—to say and allowed them the opportunity to speak; I always tried to help them at my level. If for some reason, I wasn't able to—or if the information being presented was out of the small unit leader level—I would let someone know and pass along the information. I would never make a promise that I couldn't keep or back up.

The children were also a great source of information since they would say things that the adults wouldn't. When talking to the children, I would keep in mind that they were young and would one day be fighting age. I would constantly ask my Marines what they had done to keep them from becoming the enemy?

I wanted to instill a mind-set that each of my Marines would think, *When these children are forty, what will they tell their children about Americans?* The children were impressionable, and we were careful about what we said and how we said it. The young ones could pick up on our habits quickly, and we were sure to leave them with good ones.

As time went by, the elders and children would integrate into my patrols. I had earned their trust, and they were confident in the security we had provided. I always listened to local elders and would take smaller items of gear off when talking to them. I would put out security and remove what I could in order to make them a little bit more comfortable and show them that there was a sense of security. They saw this, and they started to feel safe.

Winning the trust of the Afghan people was the cornerstone of success for our company. Establishing open lines of communication and providing security for the villagers in our area of operations surrounding Company Outpost Tohrgar allowed us to receive valuable information in our efforts to defeat the local insurgents. We wanted to defeat the enemy by using unconventional means where we didn't have to revert to our weapons as a first impulse.

Having weapons was not enough to gain the trust of the people. In order to do this, it was important that the population supported us as we worked *with* them. Taking the time to engage the local nationals and identifying their concerns and issues contributed to our efforts to gain the support of the local population. By addressing local problems, we were preparing the local nationals for independence from insurgent domination. We had to remember that it was their country; once we left, they were going to be responsible for continuing what we had left them with. They were the ones who would have to live with the results.

CHAPTER V

PSALM 91:1–16

There are no atheists in a fighting hole.
—Gunner Gilbert H. Bolton (Ret. USMC)

I kept this scripture, which I had printed on a folded cloth, inside my flak jacket under my SAPI plates; I would read it before I stepped off on patrol each day.

He who dwells in the secret place of the Most High
Shall abide under the shadow of the Almighty.
I will say of the Lord, He is my refuge and my fortress;
My God, in Him I will trust.
Surely He shall deliver me from the snare of the fowler
and from the perilous pestilence.
He shall cover me with His feathers,
and under His wings I shall take refuge;
His truth shall be my shield and buckler.
I shall not be afraid of the terror by night,
Nor of the arrow that flies by day,
Nor of the pestilence that walks in darkness,
Nor of the destruction that lays waste at noonday.

A thousand may fall at my side,
And ten thousand at my right hand;
But it shall not come near me.
Only with my eyes shall I look and see the reward of the wicked.
Because I have made the Lord, who is my refuge,
Even the Most High, my dwelling place,
No evil shall befall me, Nor shall any
plague come near my dwelling;
For he shall give his angels charge over
me, To keep me in all my ways.
In their hands they shall bear me up, Lest
I dash my foot against a stone.
I shall tread upon the lion and the cobra,
The young lion and the serpent I shall trample underfoot.
Because I have set my love upon him, therefore he will deliver me;
He will set me on high because I have known His name.
I shall call upon him, and he will answer me.
He will be with me in trouble; He will deliver me and honor me.
With long life He will satisfy me and show me His salvation.

(New King James Version Bible)

PHOTO GALLERY

Capt Day issuing us our op order before we insert

1st day on patrol in Nawa

2nd platoon, 1st squad

2nd platoon holding security

**Going over the mission with the Brits, the squad
leaders and our platoon commander**

Myself on the squad radio talking with my team leaders

ANA vic hit an IED coming to help us in a firefight

LCpl Miller and Krupa in a firefight on election day

Every day on patrol in Nawa

Basic combat load prior to stepping on a patrol

LCpl Ibanez and LCPl Barker of 1st platoon
finding humor in our AO

My terp Jimmy and platoon commander with some LNs

Stopping the poppy drug flow one bag at a time

Patrolling through a local bazaar in the market

We told the Army not to take this route

A sign of success in Nawa

LCpl Hogan laughing during a tactical pause in operations

Apache News

RIP LCpl Hogan

LtCol McCollough dressed in traditional Afghan clothes

SNCOs of NAWA

Amazing Marines

Dyer Navy Comm with Valor presented by Captain Lance Day

CHAPTER VI

YOUR NEW NICKNAME IS LUCKY

No one book or document alone can adequately prepare
you and your team for combat deployment to Afghanistan.
Each leader *must* constantly read, work, and search to locate
and collect additional useful ideas and information in this
rapidly changing theater. I challenge each leader in 1/5 to
continue to build upon the excellent base of knowledge
you and your units have achieved to date. This enhanced
level of readiness can *only* be achieved through continued
tough, realistic, repetitive, and re-mediated training.
—William F. McCollough, Commanding
Officer, First Battalion, Fifth Marines

Growing up, I watched a lot of *G.I. Joe*, America's elite counterterrorist
fighting force who would constantly battle the villainous terrorist
organization, Cobra. Their firefights were at close range, shooting
laser guns, but they never hit one another. There was just a lot of
noise and rounds downrange.

I found myself relating to this, minus the laser guns, and I felt
like a modern-day G.I. Joe cartoon when engaging the Taliban.
Aside from the fact that every intersection, bridge, water crossing,

and probably every corner was laced with IEDs, a majority of our firefights were close range, within three hundred meters and lasted no more than twenty minutes—just like G.I. Joe.

The types of firefights or TIC (troops in contact) we were involved in were mostly harassing fire, pop shots, or several quick, large bursts. Afterward, they would fall back and blend back into the local population.

Our battalion gunner, Gunner Marine (yes, that's his real last name) said, "Recognize small arms fire for what it is in accordance with the enemy's local TTPs. If it is just a few pop shots, more than likely the enemy is attempting to get a reaction from you and see what you do. They will shoot a couple shots at you, while using observers. You set up a base of fire and conduct an action left, and then two days from now, they will conduct an identical SAF attack. If you go left this time, you will quickly locate an IED the wrong way. On the other hand, if the bad guys start shooting at you like they mean it, they are there to fight. You have to be immediate in your drill if you want to fix them and kill them."

It was very frustrating to have this happen repeatedly. The primary weapon of choice in our AO was IEDs (improvised explosive devices), and they were everywhere. Some were planted prior to us arriving, and others were dug in, inserted, and connected daily as we patrolled the streets, talked with local nationals, and went about our business. It was often said in my company that getting shot at wasn't an issue. It was scary, but it was something that we could mentally overcome—and we had options. IEDs were a different story, and they scared us.

On July 25, my squad was tasked with a patrol in the northwest sector of our AO. This area was a concern because it bordered the desert and was a primary entry point for insurgents. I referred to this area as the "Land of the Lost" because it looked so abandoned. It was in the middle of nowhere; the land ended, changing from cornfields and compounds to desert for as far as the eye could see. This was the second patrol my squad had done to the area since it was the most northwestern boundary as well as the southern boundary of the unit to our north, Bravo Company.

Patrolling up there was always fascinating because it was like seeing a new area for the first time. Each time, we would push the limits and patrol a little farther away from our boundary line. On the map, a perfect triangle of land was surrounded by Routes Molson, Rolling Rock, and Tiger. We tried to stay away from Rolling Rock, which ran north and south in the western part of our AO, because it was known for IEDs.

Molson ran east and west and connected our COP (company outpost) to one of our security outposts called Five Points (because four roads led to this area, making a five-way intersection). The area that we were going to check out was called White 20, the intersection of Tiger and Rolling Rock. White 20 came from a map we used that had certain points predesignated with a white circle and a number. It was easy to reference an area based on that. White 20 was about five clicks as the crow flies and was just south of the 71 northern (boundary line designated by the grids); the 72 northern was our limit of advance.

I sat down with my team leaders to conduct a map reconnaissance and plan our route. For that patrol, I requested Hitch and Sergeant Elizondo—as I did with most—so we could take the roads in some areas. Elizondo, the point man, and I went over several routes and decided on one that took us east of Rolling Rock until we got to the intersection. From there, I wanted to push another click north, just shy of the 72 limit of advance, to check out a row of compounds.

As we approached the 72 northern and checked out every compound en route, we decided that there wasn't much going on and thought it was a good idea to head back. The route back would take us down Route Tiger since I didn't like the option of cutting through beside the road. It was tight with a few compounds and several danger areas, which is why I decided to use the road for a bit with Hitch and Elizondo leading the way.

I would often take point beside Elizondo because I liked leading from the front. Since we didn't patrol Route Tiger much, it seemed fitting to lead by example. It also allowed me the opportunity to see things from the front and get a feel for the area. Each corner, compound, alleyway, side street, or cornfield had its potential dangers, and I wanted to be up in the front where I could best observe.

About four hundred meters down on Tiger, a little side road ran to our east and connected to Rolling Rock. There were several compounds and a small cornfield in the area just ahead of me. I grabbed my map and opened it up like a newspaper. I showed Elizondo the road on the map and suggested turning down the road to check out some of the compounds. Then we could head directly south and hit Molson.

Just as I began to fold up my map, a loud explosion erupted. Boom! An IED went off directly to the left of us, about forty feet from our position in the cornfield. My head felt as if it had been slapped a hundred times, and my ears were ringing.

The explosion rocked the patrol, and dust quickly filled the air. We couldn't see anything around us. As soon as the explosion happened, I dropped the map. Elizondo and I looked up to where Hitch was sniffing about thirty feet in front of us. It was all dusty, and we couldn't see anything.

I immediately looked back at my fire teams and saw movement. Team leaders were shouting to me that there were no injuries. Everyone was okay.

Bounds and Martinez started to maneuver in an attempt to start to cordon the area. Camacho's fire team immediately turned to the right and started to maneuver toward the single compound on the other side of the road. They were doing what we rehearsed and trained for. They used the 5 Cs: confirm (was it an IED or another type of explosion), clear (leave the immediate area as detonation may be imminent by secondary devices), call, cordon (establish a perimeter of about three hundred meters) and control (maintain visual with eyes or binoculars and observe to see any enemy activity of persons fleeing).

"Holy shit, E. You okay?" I asked as we waited for any sight of Hitch.

"I think so. I can't see Hitch. Hitch. Here boy. Come!" he yelled.

After a few seconds, we were still in shock, standing in the middle of the road. I couldn't figure out how in the hell an IED could go off and cover us in dust and we could still be there.

All of a sudden, Hitch walked back toward us. He was covered in gray dust and wagging his tail. He looked like he knew he had found an IED. *Look at me. Look at me. I found an IED, guys!*

"What the hell just happened?" I asked Elizondo as we started to move toward cover. As the dust settled, I started to see better. There was a crater in the ground, and a giant section of the trail was missing. Near the blast sight, the corn was ripped through like cell phone service bars going from shortest to tallest. When it occurred to me what had just happened, I got the radio and called in the IED report to the COC. "COC, this is 2-1. Stand by for POSREP and IED 9 line. No MEDEVAC will be needed at this time. Over."

"2-1, wait one. Apache 6 wants to talk to you. Over."

I wonder what the CO wants. He doesn't take combat reports. Oh crap. I bet he is going to be pissed that we crossed the 71 boundary line and went to the limit of advance. Wait for it.

"Hey, 2-1, it's six. Is everyone okay? We heard the blast back there, but we can't see anything with the GBoss. Just smoke and dust."

"Yes, sir. Everyone is okay." I let out a sigh of relief. "Minor headaches and some ear ringing, but we got lucky."

"Okay, roger. Let us know if you need anything additional. Here's COC. Six out."

"2-1, send your traffic. Over."

"COC IED report as follows break, time now, current location IVO four hundred meters south of White 20, 41RPQ1970-7053, 2-1 was hit by an IED, no injuries. Break. IED appeared to be buried. It looks like a directional fragmentation (DF) command detonated, intended for a dismounted patrol. HME (homemade explosives) in what appears to be a pressure cooker. Break. Five Cs (confirm, call, clear, cordon and control) being conducted, and we are currently searching the area for any persons of interest. Mission RTB time has been impacted, request one-hour extension. Over."

"2-1, that's approved. Tango. Please send SITREP into COC if anything changes. Over."

"Solid copy. 2-1 out."

Sending information back takes time, and it meant a lot of radio traffic for talking with my team leaders and COC. While I was calling in the report, Camacho called me over the squad net and said he was questioning a male and needed me over there. Our conversation was typical. Through my terp, I asked him what his name was, where he lived, and what he was doing.

He said, "This is my house, and I am heading home after going to the market."

Instantly, this struck me as odd for several reasons. He wasn't carrying anything, the market was about seven clicks away, and he was walking, not driving.

I looked at him and said, "I think one of two things just happened. Either someone told you to stay out of your house because they were using it as a place to watch our patrol—or you are the triggerman who just set off the IED and are trying to get back to your home before we catch you."

He said he didn't know about any IED, he didn't hear an IED, and he didn't know what I was talking about.

The conversations became a circle of wasted time, and he was driving the bus.

I took his photo, his name, and the location of his compound and went back to the IED spot. Looking at the blast spot, I came to two possible conclusions: Somebody was watching our patrol and put in an IED or we surprised them when we came around the bend in the road. They put it in quickly, aiming it in the wrong direction, and they blew it once we came into sight. This would explain why the blast and fragmentation went into the cornfield.

The second possibility was that the little pricks knew we avoided roads and used the little trails parallel to the cornfields. This would explain why the IED was placed almost on the path, aiming into the corn, which would have completely amputated the lower legs if someone was hit. The direction of the blast and how it cut the corn stalks was aimed up. I went with option two that this DF IED was targeting our dismount patrol, hoping we would hit it. I chuckled a little when I realized this and told Camacho we got lucky again.

We looked the area over for any type of evidence, gathered up some shrapnel from the IED, and put it into some plastic bags for our intel cell to look at. As we started to make our way over to the little side road, I noticed footprints near the blast area. They looked fresh, and they were moving away from a spot in the ground where it looked like someone had been lying down.

"Bounds, look at this." His fire team was my tactical search team, and Bounds was pretty savvy when it came to combat hunter, tracking, and profiling. "Doesn't this look like someone was lying here, watching us, detonated the IED, and then casually walked away in that direction." I pointed down the road toward a compound.

"It sure does. I bet he set the IED off, and we couldn't see him walk away with all of the dust and confusion. Let's go check out that compound."

I took Jimmy, Elizondo, Hitch, and Bounds down on the little side road and put the other fire teams out to the flanks. We utilized our combat hunter tracking skills, took some photos of the prints, and followed them. They were Skechers shoes and about a size 9. The prints came out from the compound and led directly to the spot where a triggerman could have sat—and then they led directly back into the compound.

I spotted a guy in dark clothing running from the compound, and then he disappeared into the cornfield. I pushed Camacho's team out into the field to flank him.

Martinez and the remainder of Bounds' fire team flanked around the back of the compound and set up an inner cordon. I took the group I was with and ran straight for the compound. The terp yelled out, asking if anyone was home, and another male walked out.

I had Jimmy ask about the man who was running from the compound. He, of course, didn't know who we were talking about.

I asked if anyone else lived there, and he said his brother did but wasn't home. I was not surprised that he didn't hear any explosions or know anything about the IED. A different day, another LN, same circle.

Camacho came over the squad net and said, "Hey, there is a little shack over there. As soon as we came out of the cornfield, about three people ran inside. Want my team to push up and check it out?"

"Yeah. Hey, let's move out and check that place out. After, let's RTB. We have been out way too long, and Hitch is pretty much done." I was getting frustrated. Talking with the LNs was almost pointless, or so it seemed so far. They didn't know us, we didn't know them, and we had only been there a few weeks. We'd had IEDs and random firefights, yet we couldn't even locate the enemy. The LNs wanted protection from the Taliban, but they claimed not to have seen any Taliban in a while. In the same sentence, they'd say that the Taliban came into their village at night and threatened them. I felt as if I'd just been through eight hours of storytelling and dodging IEDs.

As we approached the small hut, I set up an inner cordon and an outer cordon. Once they were set, I moved in. Since I didn't know what to expect, we came in muzzle up in case anybody wanted to do us harm. It was a small, square mud-wall hut with sticks and branches for a roof. It had tin doors and some curtains. It was similar to what I had blown into with the C-4.

Jimmy, Elizondo, and I went inside and found seven teenagers. There were no AK-47s or RPGs this time. The shack had a little bit of everything: electronics, cell phones, cameras, cigarettes, sodas, drink mixes, and snacks. We entered pretty aggressively and probably startled them.

I was irritated, frustrated, and tired. I wanted nothing more than to catch the guy who had set off the IED. I yelled, "What do you know about the IED? Who did it? Was it you?" I pointed to one of them.

They were so scared and screaming back at me. For all I knew, they were saying, "Go fuck yourself, you infidel."

My terp was in the middle, trying to translate at the rapid rate.

Elizondo couldn't take it. He was laughing hysterically and called over a few of the Marines to witness what I was doing.

"Who set the IED off? If I find out it was you, you will never see your friends again!"

My terp struggled to keep up, and I was in their faces. It was aggressive, but I was not doing this out of humor. I was so fed up that the basic methodology of tactical questioning was out the door. "What are these? Cell phones? Are you calling the Taliban? Huh?"

I continued to yell random questions. I suddenly stopped, turned to Jimmy, and gave him some money. I told him to get us four ice cold zamzams and a few packets of drink mix.

The look on their faces was priceless. Two seconds earlier, I had been yelling, and just like that, I asked for some orange soda and drink mix. I walked out of the store and sat down on a cement block. I passed out the orange zamzams and drink mixes, and we relaxed as the sun started to set. We reminded one another how lucky we were to have avoided that IED. The day could have turned out very differently.

I popped open the zamzam and took a sip. At that moment, I was reminded of something our battalion commander had told us before we inserted. He'd said, "No one book or document alone can adequately prepare you and your team for combat deployment to Afghanistan."

He was spot on.

CHAPTER VII

PB JINGLE BELLS

The Marine Corps might screw you, and your girlfriend or wife
might leave you, and the enemy might kill you, but the shared
commitment to safeguard one another's lives is unnegotiable
and only deepens with time. The willingness to die for another
person is a form of love that even religions fail to inspire,
and the experience of it changes a person profoundly.
—Sebastian Junger, *War*

August 20, 2009

I was sitting inside the COC of PB Jingili, which was one of two
company outposts. We called it PB Jingle Bells because nobody
could pronounce the name correctly. We were looking over the map
of our battalion's AO. It was something I would do each day to stay
familiar with our battle space. However, on that day, it wasn't for
map reconnaissance.

It was the second presidential election under the present
constitution of Afghanistan, which involved incumbent Hamid
Karzai and his main rival, Abdullah Abdullah. Hamid Karzai had
won the elections in 2004.

All morning and into the afternoon, the radio was flooded with contact reports of firefights and IEDs from adjacent units to our north. I heard Bravo Company troops in contact; PB Baker under attack, our Battalion Command Post was under attack, Weapons Company in contact. Looking at the map of the whole area, it was clear the enemy was moving south, attacking every patrol and every base along the way. They were systematically working their way south, almost every hour on the hour.

"COC Main, this is PB Outlaw. I mean Jingili. This is 2-1 actual. Over."

"PB Jingili, this is Torghar. Apache 5 advises you to use proper call signs when calling over the net. PB Outlaw is no longer—and will be called PB Jingili. Over."

It always drove me nuts to call over the radio to our company post. Those damn radio call signs for our outposts drove me nuts. I suppose it was because we had operated just fine without them for almost two months. Then one day, our platoon commander informed us that the main company post was no longer Apache; it was Torghar. The outpost we were currently at was no longer PB Outlaw; it was PB Jingili. The one to our southeast where the ANA stayed was PB White Horse.

"Yeah, got it. Are you guys tracking these firefights that have been going on all morning? Are you seeing what I am seeing? I think this PB is next. Over."

"Affirm. We have been marking the TICS and updating the COC map. Over."

"Okay … so … do you have any guidance for us if we are attacked? I want to remind you as you sit comfortable in your COC that I am here with a squad minus because 2 Actual (platoon commander) and 2 Bravo (platoon sergeant) have second and third squads-break-securing routes for the election and they won't be back RFL (return to friendly lines) until 1900. Over."

"Yes. We copy all and are aware. Apache 5 says due to your small numbers, you are to remain standing your posts and not to DFL (depart friendly lines) for any reason unless reinforcement comes or otherwise directed. Over."

"Got it. 2-1 actual out."

Sounds like an awesome plan! I wasn't too excited about leaving the PB manned with the numbers we had to begin with, but the CO wanted other missions accomplished that day. I don't think anyone expected this wave of attacks, and if they did, it was poorly communicated. I could see from the perspective of the Taliban that attacking our positions on election day was a sign of force and a win for them. Perhaps they hoped this would intimidate the people by displaying that the US forces couldn't stop them. I thought it was clever and tactically executed.

I walked the PB with my team leaders. Camacho, Bounds, and Martinez checked the positions again. We had a two-man post on the southern entrance that covered the main avenue of approach into our PB. We had another post on the northeastern corner of the building that was manned by one man during the day and two at night. On the roof looking west, we had a two-man position. A one-man post on the southwestern corner of the PB could hop on the MK-19 or 50 caliber mounted on the HMMWV that was positioned alongside the post at any time.

We walked around each one, and made sure that the Marines were good and were manning the posts in accordance to my standards. My squad was the only squad at the PB; the rest of the platoon, the platoon sergeant, and the platoon commander were securing routes and setting up blocking positions as a company effort.

Each PB was maintained by about a squad-sized element. I had just enough to man each position for about eight hours, leaving the team leaders, a few weapon attachments, and me to spare. We could sustain it for twenty-four hours, but it would be pushing us all to our limits. Our mission was to keep the PB secure at all costs until the remainder of the platoon RTB (returned to base). At that point, we would continue with our normal post rotation and COC watch hours.

The evening was slowly approaching. It was nearing five o'clock. Nothing was out of the ordinary, besides the firefights trickling down our way. The day was ending just as quickly as it started.

I was talking with the Marines on one of the posts about anything unusual they may have seen. The two-man post was responsible for all vehicles and foot traffic that crossed through, and it had a direct line of sight down into town, which was about five hundred meters away. The nearest compound was about four hundred meters to the west. Behind the compound, there was a series of small shacks and shops. In the fields, the corn was at its peak. The stalks reached twelve feet.

All of a sudden, a sharp crack sound, *crack, crack, crack,* came from the front of our PB. One of the Marines from the roof called over the radio and said that they had received three rounds of incoming fire.

Several seconds passed, but there were no more shots. It almost appeared as a single three-round burst pop shot. I grabbed my radio and I ran over to the roof.

"All posts report anything you see that looks unusual or appears to be out of the ordinary. Roof post just received a small burst from the west. Follow all ROEs and return a high volume of fire when receiving fire in all cases."

Once I got up to the top of the roof, I moved over to the M240B, which Lance Corporal Allen was manning.

"Hey, Allen, did you see anything? Send me an ADDRAC!" This was a term used to send the firefight information, alert, direction, description, range, assignment and control.

"I didn't. I was looking around, scanning, and all of a sudden, the wall in front of us took several shots. I didn't see anything. I couldn't even return fire because I had no idea where it was coming from."

I looked down in the direction that the fire could have come from. It was very quiet in the market area, and I couldn't see anybody outside—let alone anyone who could have fired at us. I started to think it had just been a test to see how we reacted. The Taliban often did that to us, especially when it involved IEDs.

I climbed back down off the roof and went back to the post I was on. I looked back down toward the direction of the market and still saw nothing. There was the possibility that it had come from the cornfield. If someone was firing at us, we would not be able to locate him or detect him easily. *Crack, crack, crack!* Another burst rang out. I raised my M4 up and looked through my optics. I immediately saw an individual pop out around the corner of the compound.

"All posts be advised shots coming from the lone compound directly to our west approximately four hundred meters. All posts maintain security and cover your sectors."

Just as I passed that info out, more shots came my way. I returned fire at the individual.

Another guy came out around the corner, then another and another. They ran across the road and into the canal. Just as that happened, there was a loud boom near post four, which was located out back and watching the northeast part of our PB.

"Post 4 is receiving small arms fire. We have three individuals in the cornfield near the stream. We just blew claymore one!"

I chuckled to myself while thinking about them blowing the claymore mine. I ran over to post two, which was located next to the 50-caliber machine gun on the HMMWV. Lance Corporal Krupa and Lance Corporal Miller were already engaging the enemy from the corner of our PB. They were not even on post, but they ran out in flip-flops, cammie bottoms, and their Kevlar flak jackets. They were great Marines, and this didn't surprise me at all.

I told Lance Corporal Guerro to jump up on the 50-caliber machine gun and open her up. Guerro jumped up onto the 50 caliber and started returning fire at the compound.

He and I coordinated over the radio to control the fires of the 50 caliber and the M240 machine gun on the roof while he ran from gun to gun. He let out a few twelve-round bursts and then jumped back down. He ran up to the roof and helped direct fire with the other machine gunner on the M240B. He continued this for the whole duration of the firefight, running back and forth to ensure that his machine gunners had enough ammo and were on target.

I was firing back from post two, from beside the HMMWV. Miller had an M203 and yelled, "I see one individual in the road."

I moved my optic over, and as soon as I saw him, Miller pulled the trigger on the M203, sending a 40mm grenade in his direction. Boom! Through my optic, I saw an enemy fighter firing at us from the road one second, and the next second, his upper torso dissipated into a pink mist.

Miller hit him directly in the chest from four hundred meters away and blew him in half.

"Nice hit!" Miller yelled.

"That was insane. Nice shot!" I said.

I left that post and climbed up to the roof to post three. From the roof, Bounds told me that he had been firing at three men in what he believed was a machine gun position. They had seen eight enemy fighters in the compound. From my position, I was exposed, but I was doing my best to keep a lower profile. I yelled over to Allen on the M240.

"Allen, increase your rate of fire to the cyclic rate (maximum rounds) for ten seconds, then to the rapid for ten, and then back to the sustained rate! Bounds, I need you to prep and fire your LAW while Allen and I provide suppressive fire for you!"

Bounds crawled back about five feet while Allen and I suppressed to allow Bounds to get his LAW ready to fire. Bounds came up into his firing position and boom! A second delay was followed by the impact. Boom! The firing ceased for a few seconds.

I had to take a knee to better observe any movement. The machine gun position that he fired had been eliminated. As the smoke and dust settled, a burst of fire rang out and impacted the sandbag directly in front of me. The sandbag moved and shot up dust. Crack, crack, crack—they all hit just below me.

I immediately fell into a prone position. If those sandbags hadn't been there, the rounds would have hit me directly in the hip and gut. I climbed back down off the roof and ran over to post four. They were maintaining their security and hadn't seen anything since the initial firefight. I checked all the posts. Each post was on the outside of the compound and was protected by sandbags. We spent days, weeks, and every second we could to build and make solid fighting positions—and they were working well. Running between the posts, I was exposed multiple times to enemy fire. I wasn't concerned about getting hit, but it was definitely a possibility.

Meanwhile, up on the roof we were still engaging the enemy and about fifteen minutes had gone by. I wanted to take a team of four to flank the enemy coming through the high corn to the west and turn into them flanking them from the south. We were in a perfect spot to do so, but I hesitated on this action for a few minutes. I thought it over and decided not to split up my squad. Although we were equipped to do so, if something happened, we did not have the capabilities to send out a quick reaction force without seriously jeopardizing our PB security. As I was weighing the options, the COC main called me over the net.

"PB Jingili this is COC main. Over."

"COC main, go for 2-1. Over."

"Be advised 2-2 reports an ANA vehicle with three packs heading north on Keystone toward your position. They just passed our pos and should be there shortly. We do not have comm with them, and at that point, cannot confirm nor deny they are in fact ANA. Over."

"Roger. Solid copy. I have eyes on now. They are about seven hundred meters out from the market. Over."

"Okay. COC main out."

We could see the vehicle and dust trail coming up Keystone. The vehicle was definitely hauling ass. Through my optics, I could make out a passenger, driver, and one ANA in the back of the truck in the up gun position. The vehicle disappeared briefly as it went in and out of the trees along Keystone, obstructing my view.

Out of nowhere, the craziest thing that I have ever seen happened. To this day, it still takes the cake. Boom! It was the largest explosion I have ever seen. The ANA vehicle hit an IED planted on Keystone. The truck split into two, and the up gunner was blown at least fifty feet in the air.

From the roof, I could see the body soaring in the air over the trees and across the road. It disappeared behind the compounds on the other side of Keystone. It was a very disturbing sight. Part of the truck flew almost as high and went over the trees into the cornfield. It didn't look good from where I was watching.

"COC main, this is 2-1. Over."

"PB Jingili, send it for COC main. Over."

"The ANA vehicle just struck an IED on Keystone about two hundred meters south of the market intersection. How far out is 2-2? We do not have the numbers to send out a team. Over."

"2-2s last known position was west of Keystone, about a click south of your position. Apache 6 says to maintain your security and do not leave the PB. Over."

"Roger. Solid copy. 2-1 out."

When the dust settled, I was still in shock. I had never seen anything like the two-door Ford pickup getting blown up like that—and the body flying through the air. It wasn't much longer that the firefight stopped. We maintained our posts, locking in on our sectors.

I called around to all the posts to check if they could see any movement. Each post saw nothing.

The Marine in post one called in and said, "I got movement. I have what appears to be one ANA soldier coming east toward our position."

From the roof, I could see what he was talking about. I looked through my optics and saw that the man's uniform was ripped. His face was bloody, he was covered in dirt, and he was limping. I wanted to exit the compound and go help him. I wanted to send a team out there to bring him back in. I was amazed that anyone was even alive in that marketplace. I was pretty sure he had survived the IED blast.

He made his way up to post one, and I was waiting for him with our corpsman and our terp. We brought him inside, and his wounds were surprisingly minor. He had a few cuts on his leg and a several little cuts on his arms. His ears had blood in them, and his nose was bleeding. The corpsman and I worked on him as the terp tried to get his story.

He had been at the other PB and heard over the radio that we were in a firefight. He and two others took a vehicle and drove up to help. Everyone told him not to because they said it might be an ambush. When they hit the IED, the truck was split and his brother, the up gunner, was ejected and the passenger was thrown from the vehicle. Both of them were dead. He was knocked unconscious for a short period and then made his way up to our PB. He wanted us to help him to get his ANA soldiers.

I explained how we didn't have enough Marines to leave and provide enough security for two places until another squad returned. After listening to his story, I realized that the Taliban probably attacked our PB in the hopes that we would send a reaction force to help from Tohrgar. They planted an IED on the road for that reaction force. The ANA were the unlucky ones that particular day.

When 2-2 came back onto the wire, we quickly debriefed them. I took my squad and departed PB Jingili, heading down into the market with my terp. While 2-2 provided cover for us, we headed toward the marketplace. EOD called and told us to go there and secure the area so they could come in to examine the IED and look for others.

In the marketplace, I set up a perimeter and covered all the avenues of approach. I took Corporal Bounds' team and started to search the area on the west side of the canal. The front part of the truck was on the east side of the road about thirty meters from the IED blast. The back half of the truck was on the opposite side of the road, facing the opposite direction, about thirty meters from the blast sight.

As we looked on the west side, Corporal Bounds yelled, "I see a boot. It looks like the boot from one of the ANA soldiers." He moved closer. "Oh shit! There is a foot still inside it. I have a boot and a foot!"

There was a hand about five feet away, and I was pretty sure they all belonged to the same soldier. In the small stream just ahead of me, I saw the ANA soldier. I walked over to where I could see more clearly, and it was just his upper torso. Part of his face and his left hand were missing. It was the up gunner. His lower body was found about thirty feet away. Sadly, the other ANA soldier who had been ejected was dead too. At least he was in one piece.

It wasn't the first time—or the last time—that IEDs would take the lives of those we partnered with. IEDs targeted anyone and anything without care. They never looked back—and they were unpredictable. As I helped clean up body parts and collect gear, I thought about our battalion commander's advice. *No one book or document alone can adequately prepare you and your team for combat deployment to Afghanistan.*

CHAPTER VIII

A TRUE TEST OF FAITH AND TACTICS

An ear bleeding blast rocked us all. I lay flat on my back.
Eyes open but only dust and smoke fill the air. I choke
on the taste of gunpowder and blood. Slowly and one by
one the groans of pain and fear break the silence.
—Corporal Rocky Hoard, United States Marine Corps

August 25, 2009

Almost a week had gone by since the elections, and things were shifting toward holding and stability operations. The hot summer months made it extremely challenging to conduct even the simplest security patrols, and Marines prayed for night patrol. Although nights in August were still above 100 degrees, during the day it often hit 135.

My squad was tasked with an 0200 patrol down south to set up an LP/OP (listening post/observation post) in an area we called the Pinjado District—the Khosrbad area to the Zarest village—which was about six clicks south of our COP. We knew about the patrol the day prior and would depart friendly lines at 0200, inserting around 0300.

There was a lot of Taliban activity between 0100 and sunrise. The reason for heading there was that the day before the election, August 19, several Taliban fighters came into the village at night and beheaded two government elected officials (GEO), Abdul La Khan and Muhammad Anwar. The Taliban told the family that they would come back and kill everyone if anyone talked.

Our mission was to sneak into the area at dark and set up the LP/OP and wait until morning broke around 0800. We would do these often, and the goal was to move undetected in the darkness, set up, and observe the area with our night optics and thermal heat optics. Ideally, this would allow us to prevent and catch Taliban fighters from entering the village at night and intimidating or killing the local nationals.

It was late Tuesday night, and we had the satellite phone for the night. Each platoon would get it for so many hours, and each Marine would get a chance to call home. The conversations were usually about ten to twenty minutes, with at least five of those minutes spent trying to get a connection. It was like holding your cell phone up to the sky and looking for full bars. *Can you hear me now? Can you hear me now? Move three feet to left. Can you hear me now?* It was always nice to be able to call home.

We had been operating in Helmand for almost two months, and it was only my third call home. As it approached midnight our time, which was approximately 11:30 a.m. PST, I gave the last call for anyone to use the phone. Most of my Marines were sleeping because we had a patrol in a few hours.

Lance Corporal Hogan was still up, and I said, "Hogan. Have you had a chance to call home yet to let everyone know you're okay?"

He was always a quiet one, but he would do anything he was told without looking back. He volunteered for every single assignment with enthusiasm. Before the deployment, I was his platoon sergeant while he was in my squad for a short time. This was his first deployment, and he had a reputation as a workhorse.

"No, Sergeant Dyer. I am going to wait until tomorrow. I think it's late right now."

I looked at my watch, and it was almost midnight. "Well, Hogan, you know that there is an 11.5 hour difference between us and California. I think you should at least give your parents a ring to say hi. Unfortunately, in our line of business, we are not guaranteed a tomorrow. Seek all opportunities to make a call home, even if it is a voice mail." I handed the phone to Hogan and went down to my sleeping area to look over my map. I had to start working on my overlay and combat order for the patrol in a few hours.

August 26: 0200

"COC, this is Apache 2-1. Over."

"2-1, this is COC. Send your traffic. Over."

"Yeah. Hey, this is 2-1 actual, and we have reached and inserted into checkpoint five at this time. All security is set and the LP/OP is established—break—I request a wasp to scan with IR our position in order to identify any movement coming near us. Over."

The wasp was a Micro Air Vehicle (MAV), a small, portable, reliable, and rugged unmanned aerial platform designed for day or night air reconnaissance and surveillance. It was basically a wicked cool fucking paper airplane that Sergeant Bossow, our mortarman turned company intelligence Marine, could launch by throwing it in the air and guiding it over our position. I referred to it as our eyes in the sky.

"2-1, that's a go on the wasp. COC will have that out shortly. Tango. Maintain radio communication and perform a radio check every hour on the hour. Report all CCIRs and any information as needed. Over."

"Roger. Solid copy on all, 2-1 actual out."

And just like that, we were alone by ourselves in the middle of nowhere, looking off into the darkness for Taliban fighters. Every time we got one of those missions, I attempted to turn it into an ambush by throwing M67 hand grenades at the enemy followed by an eruption of 7.62 and 5.56 gun fire.

The morning came without incident, and my squad broke down and patrolled back to the company outpost (often called the COP).

Lance Corporal Carrillo was called Daddy Yankee because shortly after he graduated from infantry training school for basic training, he was out having a good time with some other young Marines. They got into a huge car accident that would later hinder his ability to perform at the caliber he had always dreamed of. In the accident, the Daddy Yankee CD that was playing flew out of the CD player with such force that it sliced his head, penetrated his skull, and left him seriously wounded. True story!

As we returned to friendly lines, Carrillo came up to me and said, "Apache 5 wants to see you, Corporal Pouchoulen, and Corporal Hoard in the COC."

"Fuck! What does he want, Carrillo? Who took off their helmet on a patrol this time? Who is wearing white socks? Who didn't call in a checkpoint? I just came off a six-hour patrol with no sleep for twenty-four hours. Can't I just debrief, Carrillo?"

Carrillo had the heart of a lion, and all he wanted to do was patrol with us and do his job as an infantryman. He was always getting yelled at because he was the messenger boy inside the wire. "Carrillo, go do this, go do that, get me this, tell so-and-so to come here, etc." It was rather comical at times.

"I don't know, Sergeant Dyer. He just sent me over here to get you and the other squad leaders."

I dismissed my squad and rounded up the two other squad leaders. Corporal Hoard was standing atop a mountainous pile of dirt that he seemed to be pretty proud of. He had a pickax over his shoulder and was wearing nothing but green silkies. The trademark of any real Marine, those skintight green silky shorts left nothing to the imagination.

"Rock," I yelled as I started to laugh, "XO wants to see the squad leaders. Grab Pancho, and let's see what's up. He is probably going to yell at us because you are out here looking like the star character from *Lord of the Flies,* and all your slaves are down below digging who knows what."

"No way, dude." He waved me over and pointed down into our platoon fighting hole. "While you guys were gone, McHugh, Gentry, Gibson, and I dug a little something for Lance Corporal Hogan. Yesterday while we patrolled down to Five Points to do a resupply, old Hogan noticed a dead goat floating in the canal. He was worried that the goat would float downstream to where we bathe and contaminate the water. So he handed me his M-4 and said, 'Hold this. I am going in.' Damn Hogan went to man land, Dyer. He grabbed that dead goat by the head and dragged it up the bank. I had never seen anything like that. Man land isn't easy to get to, but old Hogan did it."

I was cracking up. If there was one thing Hoard could do better than being a Marine, it was tell stories. He would crack me up daily.

"So we dug him a private fighting hole with his own spiral staircase leading to it. Take a gander at that beauty."

Sure enough, those idiots had dug about five feet deep and carved out a spiral dirt staircase leading to a personal fighting position for Hogan as a reward for going to man land.

We all walked over to the COC and sat down with the XO. He walked us over to the oversized map that was covered in blue, red, white, and yellow tacks. It was his tracker board, and it scared us. When this happened, we always got nervous. I thought, *I wonder which twelve-click pointless movement he feels like giving us today.* As we all looked at one another, I could tell Rock and Pancho were thinking the exact same thing.

"HET has just received credible information of an IED being implanted around First Platoon's AO on Keystone near the intersection of White 12 and Old English. He doesn't have the exact place as he is still talking with the local national now. Which one of you wants the patrol to go confirm or deny any IEDs on Keystone?"

I looked over at Rock and then at Pancho. "I will go. My guys are all geared up, and I bet they haven't even put their weapons down yet. We will take it."

Rock immediately jumped in. "Nope. Sounds like a job for 2-3. We have been on rest for the last eight hours. Your guys just came off a patrol, and Pancho's guys are on post. You take a rest, and my guys will go out."

Pancho and I looked at each other and agreed. "Sounds good to me, brotha."

Pancho and I walked the posts to check on the Marines while 2-3 geared up and departed friendly lines with Elizondo and Hitch, Corporal Hoard, Lance Corporal Gentry, Lance Corporal Corson, Lance Corporal Gibson, Lance Corporal McHugh, Lance Corporal Hogan, and Hoard's terp, Sunny. It was another normal patrol that was looking for IEDs through the streets of Nawa.

> "Apache 2-3, this is Apache 5. Over."
> "Go for 2-3. Over."
> "Be advised we have a report of another possible IED in your area—break—push north up route

Keystone and see if anything looks to be unusual. Over."

"Roger, Apache 2-3 copies all. Over."

"Apache 5. Out."

"Son of a bitch!" I said.

Cody Gibson, my third team leader, knew my look of disgust. "What's the problem boss?"

"Just the typical officer mission," I replied. "Trying to win the war with a map and a radio. Looks like we need to go stomp around Helmand Province for another possible IED."

After making it to the far north intersection of Route Keystone, I held up the squad of ten Marines. The sweat was pouring out of me in the stifling Afghan sun. I know Hitch had to be feeling the heat. He was invaluable though. The ability to sniff IEDs had saved many Marines on many occasions.

Cody made his way over to me and said, "So … where are we, boss?"

We both smiled, but really meant *shut the fuck up and get us home quickly.* "Apache 2-3, Apache 2-3. This is Apache 5. Back clear Keystone and return to base. Over."

"Aye-aye, sir. Flip a bitch, fellas." I knew to never go back the way you had gone. I also understood direct and instant obedience to orders. Nothing seemed out of the usual for that godforsaken place though. Kids were out to look at the infidels patrolling the streets. Farmers were tending their fields. Everything seemed peaceful and hot.

Just a kilometer shy of base, we held up to give the dog some water. I watched Hitch jump into the canal and run parallel to the road we were traveling on. I was jealous. The dog swam several laps, but he answered the sharp voice of Elizondo. As Hitch made his way up the embankment, a startled Marine in front of me shouted that he could see a wire.

As I stared at the Marine's feet in front of me, I knew we were had. *Oh shit,* I thought.

The whole time 2-3 was on patrol, I had my gear on, and my radio was still broadcasting the communication from the COC to 2-3.

Pancho and I were walking the posts and checking on the Marines as usual to make sure they were maintaining a combat mind-set, not becoming complacent and holding their sectors of fire by keeping their weapons system pointing in the direction to best cover their position.

In the post, we were checking over the range cards and ensuring that all the information was accurate and correct. Boom! Out of nowhere, the ground and the guard post we were standing in shook. We immediately looked over directly toward 2-3s position, and there was nothing except a giant cloud of black smoke and dust. I knew exactly what had happened. The question wasn't whether they had been hit by an IED—rather how many survived.

I clicked my 152 button and said, "2-3, 2-3? Rock, are you guys okay?"

No reply.

I rolled my squad radio to 153 and called him again. "2-3, anybody? Are you guys okay?"

There was a slight delay before Rock came over the net. He was extremely weak, and his voice was raspy and mixed with coughs. It sounded as if he was talking in his sleep and going in and out of consciousness. "It's not good, man. It's not good. Everybody is hit. Everybody is ... just get here. Just get here now."

And that was it—the radio went silent. I ran into the platoon's area and told my squad to get their gear on because this is a real QRF task (quick reaction force). I directed the team leaders to make a manifest and stage by the back gate. I decided not to take vehicles even though there was a possibility of needing them for a medevac. The odds were that we would just cause a bigger mess by driving them, and I was concerned about secondary IEDs.

A Marine came out of the COC and yelled, "2-3 has been hit. There is no movement from anyone, and the GBOSS shows seven Marines down with nobody moving. The whole squad is down. I think everyone might be dead."

It was not exactly what I wanted to hear, but we had no way of telling at that point. We assumed the worst and hoped for the best.

The CO and company first sergeant ran out with their gear. "Sergeant Dyer, let's go. I need your squad."

We grabbed two corpsmen, my squad, the CO, and the first sergeant and departed friendly lines on foot. I hit start on my stopwatch.

> An ear-bleeding blast rocked us all. I lay flat on my back. My eyes were open, but only dust and smoke fill the air. I choked on the taste of gunpowder and blood. Slowly and one by one, the groans of pain and fear broke the silence. The sound of rocks descending to the ground reminded me of hail

falling back home. The haze was too great, but from what I could hear, the blast was not only felt by me.

My leg had been stripped almost completely from my body. The only thing I could do is apply the tourniquet I had practiced with a thousand times before. As I squirmed my body to get up on an elbow, I noticed all my men were on the ground. No one was talking; everyone was hurting. I felt something beneath me and realize I have shit myself. I felt everything. I could see so clearly at that moment. I could smell the corn from the small field to the east and the powder from the blast. Everything seemed to be in slow motion. I looked toward the heavens and watched the wind whisk through the leaves. I had just gone through absolute hell, but I felt like I was in heaven.

Cody pulled as hard as he could to tighten my second tourniquet. I growled and squirmed in agony, but I knew it was for the best. The gush became a steady drool from my leg. I knew my time was short. I grabbed my 153 radio and called to base.

As I rolled to the company station, Cody informed me that Lance Corporal Hogan did not survive. Seven of the eight men had been hit and severely wounded. Only two could walk, but they had severe concussions. I had never been so tired in my life. It could have been the training or simply the will for man to live, but I fought sleep with all I had. It was absolute silence. Men scrambled around me in response to the blast. I heard nothing. I only felt the wind and smelled the fields of fresh-tilled earth.

The footage from the GBOSS showed two or three motionless Marines. One Marine was stumbling around like a drunk on the road. They were all directly on Keystone, almost in a tactical column. As we exited the COB, my timer was ticking fast. Seconds seemed to move twice as fast, and the minutes came quicker than they ever had. I knew that their lives depended 100 percent on how quickly we got to them and started to execute the medevac.

The challenge wouldn't be saving their lives; it was how I was going to get to them in the most direct and safest manner. The biggest obstacle was Keystone, and the biggest fear was secondary IEDs, which would have been a perfect scenario for the enemy. They could have easily waited until QRF arrived to set off a secondary IED and then ambushed us from multiple positions.

There wasn't much room to maneuver on either side of the road, and the canal separated Keystone from the tall corn stalks. Getting there on foot was going to be a task and getting them in a vehicle would be a bigger task. I decided to lead the way. I was directly beside Lance Corporal Stoner, and he had the CMD minesweeper. We would set the pace and sweep as fast as we could without disregarding the safety of the squad.

It was a difficult decision to make: Get there fast and disregard any IEDs or take our time, being cautious of IEDs, and risk taking too much time while our fellow Marines bled out and died. Once we cleared up to 2-3, I would call in for any vehicle assistance we would need. I could assess the situation more accurately at that time.

As we moved up the road, my watch kept ticking. What started out as 00:30 was now topping 04:59, 05:10, 05:11. It seemed as if it was taking forever, and all I could think about was 2-3 bleeding out while waiting for us to arrive.

"Camacho, I need you to direct your team over to the west and cover that sector." I pointed and continued to run. "Bounds, your team goes there and covers the rear and the east along with third fire team. Team leaders, you are with me. We will go directly to the casualties and start prioritizing them."

At that point, I could see exactly what was going on. It was a mess. Part of me wanted to take out my camera and take photos. It was textbook mass casualty. When we got within fifty yards, I could see Gibson and Elizondo attempting to move the wounded Marines into a consolidated area. They were both staggering, and Gibson appeared to be worse off than Elizondo.

The first person I came up onto was Lance Corporal Hogan. He was on the ground in such a manner that I could tell the IED had killed him instantly. His head was snapped back, and his face was covered in sweat, blood, and dirt. His cammies were torn, and he was covered in blood and dirt. That image has forever been burned into my brain and has never faded. There was no time to stop and mourn.

I looked up and saw Hoard on the ground with his 153 clenched in his hand. With what little strength he had left, he managed to whisper, "The sons of bitches got us. They got us good. Hogan didn't make it. Goddamn it! Get us out of here now!"

I moved past Rock, and my team leaders started to apply first aid. The whole squad was spread all over the road. They were lifeless, hardly moving, and groaning and coughing. As I made my way to the end of the patrol, Lance Corporal Corson was squirming and breathing deeply. His helmet was off, and his blouse had been ripped open. His lower left leg was covered in blood, and his pants had been blown open. It was clear that his entire left calf was missing.

As soon as I kneeled down beside him, I noticed how severe the injury was. He had deep lacerations on his shin, and the skin was torn back. His calf was blown off, and his tibia and fibula bones were exposed in several places. I immediately starting talking to him and checking his body for secondary injuries.

He said, "Did Hogan make it? Is he okay? Can I talk to him?"

As I checked his body and started to strip off his gear, I grabbed his first-aid kit and took out his tourniquet and some gauze pads. I applied the tourniquet to his leg to slow the bleeding. I took my camel-back hose and sprayed water over his calf. There was a hole in his leg where the shrapnel had gone straight through his calf.

Corson looked up at me and grabbed me. "Sergeant Dyer, I am so sorry. I didn't see it coming at all. I was rear security, and I didn't see anybody set in an IED or anything."

"Corson, no brotha. It's not your fault at all. I am sure you did everything you could have. You were trained right, and there was nothing you could have done tactically to have prevented this. Just relax, breathe, and keep responding to me." I continued to wrap his leg and clean the area.

Corson grabbed me again and pulled me in close. "I need you to do me a favor, Sergeant Dyer. I need you to take something." He reached into his flak jacket.

At that point, I was pretty sure he thought he was not going to make it and was going to give me the dreadful "Dear Wife" letter that nobody was supposed to write, but we all did. My eyes got huge, and my heart rate started to intensify. *Please don't let this be the letter. Please, please, please.* "Corson, you are going to be fine. I am sure that whatever you have, you can give them yourself."

"No! I will get in trouble; they can't know I have this."

I was confused.

Corson reached into his gear and pulled out a set of brass knuckles!

I was even more confused—but relieved. "What the hell? You do realize you're missing your calf and losing a lot of blood, and all you can think of is giving me your brass knuckles?"

"Everyone in our squad has them, but I don't want to get in trouble. Take them please."

I was amazed by the quality of Marines we had in that company—hard-charging motivators who would do anything for one another.

Lance Corporal Corson had no calf and was covered in blood after being hit by an IED. His two main concerns were the other members of his squad, specifically Lance Corporal Hogan, and his brass knuckles. Not once did he ask about his injury or yell that he was in pain, which he most likely felt would be a selfless act.

About two minutes had passed since I had started working on Corson. We had practiced combat first aid hundreds and hundreds of times, and I was very confident in my abilities to apply all types of first aid. Since applying the tourniquet, the bleeding had slowed, but it was still flowing out through the missing calf. I decided to pour quick clot into his wound. This hemostatic agent was new to me, and I was curious how it actually would work. Its purpose was to stop the bleeding completely, and I figured it would be a perfect moment to use it. I opened the packet and poured it all over Corson's leg.

"Aw shit! What the hell!" He started moving his leg and throwing punches at me. "Stop! Stop! That hurts—whatever you're doing!"

I slammed my knee even harder into his leg and held him down, wrapped up what was remaining of his calf, and moved on to the next injured Marine.

This process was repeated until all the Marines had been treated and prioritized. We then took out a poleless litter, which was used to carry Marines, and one Marine at a time started to move the wounded to the medevac site where we had requested a bird to land.

As our CO, Captain Day was organizing the medevac on the radio. He and our first sergeant were also helping move the casualties. The team effort worked as well as it could. We had rehearsed this stuff over and over and over and over—and then we did it again and again.

As a result of that one IED, six Marines and one terp were medevac'd and treated for life-threatening wounds. Lance Corporal Hogan did not make it after taking the brunt of the IED. Shrapnel that ranged from nuts and bolts to rusty sprockets the size of tennis balls blasted through 2-3 on that patrol like they were nothing. Lance Corporal Hogan's actions that day saved the lives of his Marines, and the quick response and work of my squad got the Marines treated and medevac'd in a timely manner, which saved lives.

> Hogan observed a kite string leading onto the road from an adjacent cornfield being pulled taut in an attempt to activate the improvised explosive device. Familiar with this common enemy tactic, Hogan immediately recognized that the attack was imminent and that he had only moments to react. Without hesitation, Hogan hurled his body into the nearest Marine in an effort to keep him from the effects of the imminent explosion. Hogan then turned in the direction of the improvised explosive device and placed himself in the road so that he could effectively yell verbal warnings to the rest of his squad mates. This desperate effort to warn the rest of the patrol bought the remaining Marines valuable seconds to begin moving away from the

improvised explosive device before it detonated. Mortally wounded by the explosion, Hogan's extreme act of selflessness saved a Marine's life and allowed the rest of the squad to avoid the full brunt of the fragmentation from the improvised explosive device.

Several years since that day have passed. Much has changed. Lance Corporal Hogan posthumously was awarded the Navy Cross. Lance Corporal Cody Gibson was the recipient of the Bronze Star for Valor. All were awarded the Purple Heart for wounds received from the enemy that day. I was awarded the Purple Heart and the Navy and Marine Corps Achievement Medal for Valor for actions prior in the deployment. My son, Axel Hoard, was born three days after the blast in southern Illinois. I held him for the first time in Bethesda, Maryland, at the National Naval Medical Center. It is still hard sometimes. A smell or a picture can bring it all back. I don't have the words to truly explain much of this. I know I cry when I hear the National Anthem, and that most will never understand me. And to be honest, I am okay with that. My hands are still quite shaky though.

CHAPTER IX

AFGHANISTAN IS NOT IRAQ

When the war of the giants is over, the
wars of the pygmies will begin.
—Winston Churchill

I'm no historian—and I don't claim to be an expert on either country—but what I do know is that my assessments are based on my own experience or directly from the source of a Marine who was there. It has happened to me in many conversations with those who have never been to Iraq or Afghanistan; a majority of them want to know if Afghanistan was like Iraq or vice versa.

It's an interesting question because where does one even start to explain? I could say, "Yes! Exactly like Iraq. Matter of fact, I believe I saw the same families in Afghanistan and just thought to myself they must have traveled from one shithole to another shithole."

However, it never ceases to amaze me that no matter who I am talking with, the second someone finds out that I am a United States Marine, a series of questions follows. It happens so much that it almost seems every civilian has been briefed about what to ask when meeting a Marine. *Have you deployed to Iraq or Afghanistan? How many times? What was it like?* And so on and so forth.

They often go into a story of how they know someone who knows a person who is dating a guy who is a Marine, most likely in "Special Forces," and he has been deployed to combat eight times. I always get a good laugh when I hear this. I completely understand the interest from those who have not been, and it makes perfect sense to ask someone about what they have experienced. I am not talking down to those who ask these questions; instead, I am using this opportunity to enlighten those who do not know but have the desire to learn.

Based on these series of questions and talking with many Marines about this topic, I'll answer some questions. Is Afghanistan like Iraq? My own experiences have led me to say that Afghanistan is not like Iraq, and I've listed my top 10 reasons why.

1. Afghanistan is deeply divided tribal culture with a largely uneducated population that lives in the rural countryside.
2. The central government is weak and has poor credibility because it is plagued by corruption and an inability to provide basic services.
3. The segment of the population that could help rebuild the nation has left and most likely will never return.
4. Tribal warlords are committed to regional armed power struggles that keep the nation insecure. Corruption, mismanagement, and weak federal control over the provinces undermine humanitarian aid efforts.
5. Over 50 percent of the people are illiterate, not reading or writing the two official languages Dari and Pashto. In rural areas, 90–100 percent are illiterate.
6. The average life expectancy for a man is between forty-four and forty-five years.
7. One out of five infants dies before the age of five.

8. Most people do not have access to twenty-four-hour public electricity, indoor sanitation, adequate local medical facilities, local schools, or clean water.
9. Many roads are not passable twelve months out of the year.
10. There are no railroads inside the country.

So when did this all start? This will be your Afghanistan 101 crash course. In late December 1979—when I was four months old—Russian reserve units entered Afghanistan to support a weak pro-Soviet government. During the fifties and sixties, Afghan governments had played loyalties between America and the West and the Soviet Union. For example, Lashkar Gah, the provincial capital of Helmand Province, was built by American engineers in the 1950s when they were developing the Helmand River Valley. They were unsuccessful at creating a system of dams to create an irrigation system that would benefit more farmers. The large-scale failure turned the tide toward Russia.

Afghanistan also requested military aid, which the American government was unwilling to provide. The initial Russian forces were Muslim reservists from southern republics, and many of these troops were Tajiks, Uzbeks, and Turkmen who were despised by the Pashtuns. Many reservists were anticommunist and were often suspected of being sympathetic to fellow Muslims. The Russian invasion was a unifying event. Ethnic groups that were normally unfriendly came together to claim victory for Pashtun values and Allah. Men proclaimed that they were warriors for God, Mujahideen, against a godless foreign element. The Russian Army left one million civilian casualties, and approximately four million Afghans left the country. The Russian military littered Afghanistan with land mines and unexploded ordnance; the United Nations has called it the most land-mined country in the world.

Some areas of Afghanistan are so isolated that there were several reports of US Marines encountering local nationals who honestly believed we were Russians that were still in their country. For more than a decade, we have been fighting in their country, and I have learned a tremendous amount about the country and its people. Afghanistan is one of the world's poorest countries. It is a mountainous, landlocked, semidesert nation that is roughly the size of Texas. There are thirty-four provinces, and each one is broken up into districts. For example, the area I operated out of was the Helmand Province, in the Nawa District. The geographical location and terrain make it susceptible to drought, severe winds, floods, and earthquakes. From 1995–2001, severe drought caused famine, and many Afghans became displaced in the country or refugees in neighboring countries, particularly Pakistan and Iran. Afghanistan is three hundred miles away from the ocean and relies heavily on water from the snowcapped Hindu Kush Mountain Range in the north and the Helmand River in the south. The Helmand River is the longest river in Afghanistan and one of the ten largest in Asia. The lack of developed industries and sustainable economic programs make Afghanistan a humanitarian aid nightmare.

The main ethnic groups in Afghanistan are Pashtuns, Hazaras, Uzbeks, Tajiks, Aimaks, and Baluchs. Pashtuns are the dominant ethnic group, making up 42 percent of the approximately twenty-six to twenty-nine million population. Since 1747, there have only been a few periods when the Pashtuns have not controlled the government.

Although Afghanistan is 99 percent Muslim, Pashtunwali is a more dominant way of life on the tribal level. Pashtunwali came before Islam and is a code of living much like the codes of the American Indians. The structure and belief of Pashtunwali is what makes the local tribal environment work. An individual's actions are governed by what the code requires for them to be an honorable

Pashtun man, woman, or child. Islam and Pashtunwali are so closely entwined in tribal Pashtun culture that they are considered the same—even though they are not. It is the largest ethnic group, and they have formed the Taliban core, which will remain loyal until its defeat.

The center of gravity on the tribal level is the khan. He is the elder, community leader, and wealthiest stakeholder (property, livestock, or water). His identity as khan is greater than being a mujahideen leader. He is more concerned with maintaining his family (clan or tribe) than being part of a global jihad.

The malik is a leader with a high position who oversees administration of local affairs, and the mesher is a local tribal elder (most often over a group of families or one large single one). A mullah is a local religious leader who presides over births, deaths, and marriages. His role is not as significant as in more educated Muslim countries. Generally, they are not scholars of the Holy Qu'ran. Islam in Afghanistan is also influenced by Sufism, a type of mysticism that directs followers to achieve closeness with God through various rituals, meditations, and lifestyles. This is not mainstream Islam and is rejected by more conservative Sunni Islam believers.

The Pashtuns were particularly opposed to the Soviet-sponsored government's land reform policies. They believe they are the rightful rulers of any Afghan state, going back to 1747 when Abdur Rahman Durrani forcefully consolidated power. Hazaras, Tajiks, Uzbeks, and Turkmen were opposed to the Pashtun mujahideen who became warlords and waged civil war after the Soviets left the country. Tajiks became the backbone of the Northern Alliance, a militia who fought the mujahideen warlords and later the Taliban. The Pakistani government supported seven exiled political groups during the Russian campaign. When the Russians retreated, these groups returned to Afghanistan to claim control over Kabul and the government.

For the first time, Kabul became a battleground; a new wave of refugees left the city and the country. Violence, corruption, and lawlessness prevailed. The population wanted peace and were led to believe it would come from yet another group from Pakistan. These armed men called themselves Talib (short for Taliban), seekers of knowledge. They claimed they wanted to restore Afghanistan to a properly functioning Islamic society. Despite their promises of justice, the Talibs were primarily young, uneducated men who had been force-fed distorted history and Islamic doctrine in religious schools throughout western Pakistan. They were set loose on cities and told to restore them according to their madrasa (religious training school) instruction. They had no experience in government administration and enforced a strong set of old-fashioned interpretations of Islam. They had seized control of more than 90 percent of Afghanistan by 2001 before they were run out of the country.

The Pakistan Taliban are primarily Pashtun as well. They took refuge in the border regions with other Pashtuns and lay in wait to train, plan, and execute attacks wherever they chose. Their weapon systems range from individual AK-47s and hand grenades to crew-served/heavy weapons such as the MANPAD-SAM rocket launcher, RPG-7, 122mm mortar and 122mm rockets, DShK heavy machine guns, RPK medium machine guns, and 107mm rockets.

Their rural philosophy is based on religious conservatism, and their urban philosophy is based on secular progressive ideals. In order to establish local power, they do so by determining the dominant philosophy of each religion. The rest is history.

CHAPTER X

LESSONS LEARNED AT THE STRATEGIC AND TACTICAL LEVELS

Winners practice until they get it right—champions
practice until they can't get it wrong!
—Norman W. Davies

Weapons: 50-caliber MGs don't penetrate mud walls. Despite how many rounds you throw downrange, the SLAP or the API-T will not do it. These walls are often eight to twelve feet high and about twelve to eighteen inches thick. They are built to last. Do note, however, that I am sure the structure of these walls change AO to AO. So what is invincible to a 50 caliber in one AO may not be the same in another. The only weapon that has been successful at the small unit level was the MK-19. It makes a mess of the wall, but it will break it down. Our AO was tight. Collateral damage was a real possibility in most firefights. The 50 caliber is a great weapon, but in some cases, it can do more harm than good. Besides, why waste the rounds shooting at a wall? Save them for better targets.

MK-19

This weapon system was great in all cases. Many after actions from other units and Marines I have talked with have reported that the enemy calls this weapon the "big grenade thrower." It is the one weapon they are scared of. In a successful COIN environment, you have to be cautious of your area and what is around. This weapon alone is intimidating, and the enemy does not like it. Just be careful of collateral damage.

LAAWs

I preferred this to the SMAW. It was lighter, easier to carry, easier to use, and only required a gunner. It only took a day at the range to train up several Marines, and that created a ripple effect with the other Marines. A time-efficient rocket just made more sense. I think that each squad should carry at least one or two on every patrol. One of our squads fired two at different engagements. I don't think the enemy enjoyed that too much since their fire decreased after it impacted. Just be sure to take your used rocket with you. One weapons cache had an expended rocket.

SMAW

I've never had the opportunity to fire one. Although Marines were cross-trained on this weapon, that does not make them experts on it while being shot at. It required a different type of fine motor skills than at a relaxed range during training. The 0351s were integrated into the line platoons, but they couldn't be everywhere.

Again, the LAAW proved to work better. Besides, boresighting and always ensuring your weapon is accurate is tedious.

Mortars

Our squads carried the 60mm M224, with the M8 baseplate firing it by hand. It was light and could be a great asset in a firefight. Cross-training was simple; it only took a few hours in the rear and then some refresher classes every so often. At one point, we had our cook attachment trained on the weapon system, and he carried it on patrols. It was used once in a firefight and proved to be a great way to get some suppressive rounds downrange, which I think is all you will use it for. Suppress the enemy, then fire, move, and communicate like infantry does. Also, it allows for you to have illumination at your disposal. Finally, there is no need to wait around for approval because the company 60s can get cleared at the company level.

81s

We kept a section of guns at our COP. Other than the first day, which HE was used, the remainder of the time it was illumination missions. I think in a different AO, the 81s would be a great asset. Approval time took longer because it had to be cleared at the battalion level, even for illumination missions. By the time you were cleared, the enemy in some cases was already long gone.

M4, M16

The basic load out for these seemed to be five or six thirty-round magazines. Many Marines started out with eight or ten full magazines. I think it made sense if you were in a heavy firefight each time you left the wire, but we were not. Other than the first few days, there was no need for all that ammo. It just weighed you down. Besides, it was just more things to clean and maintain. The weapon systems worked fine. I had no issues. Keep it clean, keep the bolt lubed, and constantly ensure that you are keeping the maintenance up on them. As for the BZO, boresight the optics. Once a month, run a BZO range. That will take care of your RCO/ACOGs. Set up a place where you can do the laser boresight and BZO the PEQ 15s and 16s. Although I never used my nighttime optics and devices to assist me in winning an engagement, you never know. Always keep them sharp. I heard a lot of talk from Marines that the standard 5.56 (M855-62 grain) round we used was not good enough. We need 7.62, something with stopping power. I am not an expert, so I don't have a major opinion, but I believe that if you shot your target center mass, and take the time to aim in, your enemy will have a bad day. I would not want to jeopardize the distance and accuracy of my M16/M4 for a bigger round. I think the round works just fine.

MK-12

I never used one, but the designated marksmen said it was well worth the time and money put into these. I agree. The 77-grain round being a little bit heavier helped to produce tighter groups. Each squad should have at least one DM with them. It's great to put into place and then bound while he is the over watch. I witnessed one of my DMs at night with little illum and cloud coverage, while winds at about fifteen miles per hour, from a distance of five hundred meters using a Individual Weapon Night Sight-Thermal (IWNS-T) and his MK-12. He fired off two shots, and one of them hit the IED emplacer. BZO was simple as well. Once a month, just set up a range—and you're good to go.

M203

It was used in all the firefights. Since most of them were less than three hundred meters, it was well in range of some 40mm HE. The enemy was not a fan of our grenade weapon systems. They would hide, take cover, stop firing, or turn their fires into inaccurate pop shots. The weapon system is great to have since it is both M16/M4 and 40mm grenade launcher. It is a good way to get quick, indirect fire downrange. Sometimes rounds got up in the air and landed inside the compounds. We did not use the quadrant sights, but the leaf sights worked fine, as long as it is fired within its range. For anything over four hundred meters, I think you are wasting rounds.

M249 SAW

This was always a favorite of mine. It was small, relatively light, and a great asset to have in a squad. The SAW has always been a base of fire weapon to help establish fire superiority. The basic breakdown was between four-hundred and six-hundred rounds per Marine. A majority carried a two-hundred-round drum and two one-hundred-round drums. I would say that is a good amount given our firefights. Anything more is just added weight. As always, the weapons maintenance has to happen every day or it will jam.

M240

We started out carrying one on every patrol. As the months went on, the M240 became a post weapon. The few times it was utilized on patrol in a firefight, it worked well—as long as the weapon was cleaned, and it had a good machine gunner pulling the trigger. Employed with the M249, I thought was a good alternative to not having two guns.

M9

I suppose if all else fails, it would be nice to have a pistol. In our AO, not one 9mm round was fired at an enemy combatant. Unless a dog fits that category.

- I think the majority of our weapons, all of course being organic to the small unit level, worked well for us. The other assets we had—81s, MK-19s, and 50 caliber—all worked when needed, but they were not needed more than once or twice. The moon dust was horrible, and it was always getting into our weapons systems. Constant maintenance is the only way to prevent failure of the weapon.
- Most firefights lasted no more than forty-five minutes. Some were not even classified as firefights as they were literally several small pop shots. Perhaps they were doing this to see how we would respond or move. Or maybe they were just

testing us. Very few have lasted over an hour with Marines in our AO. The ones that did were not full-out block-three war. It was heavy, and then light, heavy, light. The enemy is known to be complex at ambushes, and was reported to use the late evening (sun set against their backs to blind us) in five-to-eight-man teams. L-shaped was the most common formation, although I never really encountered that, which is not to say others did not. They want you to move toward them, allowing them to draw you in to an IED or some type of trap. This was difficult to adjust to or decide how to close with and destroy. It is natural for us to do that since that was what we did. However, the squad leader had to make a choice, and he only had a few seconds to do so. When I was a squad leader, I often chose to stay firm or maneuver around to the flanks and come in wide. Even that was scary. In most fights, they opened up with bursts of RPKs, AK-47s, and sometimes RPGs. They started off inaccurately; however, they became more accurate as the fight progressed. We saw many positions dug in throughout our AO that resembled enemy fighting positions. I am not sure if our style and methods of patrolling countered against using them or if they chose not too. Either way, they had solid machine gun capabilities and used them. Just bring the fight to them.

- IEDs. In my amateur, nonprofessional opinion, I would say they are masters at this style of warfare. They have several methods that seemed to change from time to time. The most common we saw in our AO was a type of command detonator, using a kite string that was connected to the IED. When pulled, it would enable the circuits to connect and boom! The IED would be set to hit a specific area on the suspected route, at a specific height. We called them directional fragmentation IEDs (direct frag) due to the fragmentation they used. The triggerman was always near, often hidden in the corn or around a corner. HME seemed to be the best choice. They were quick to blend back in with the local populace. They were fast and methodical. They targeted QRF with secondary, and in some cases, they targeted QRFs backup with a third or a fourth. We had up to thirteen IEDs, and several of them were daisy-chained together in one setting. Pressure-plate IEDs can have up to eighty pounds of HME, and some are pressure-plated with directional fragmentation, elevated in walls, and aimed at dismounted troops sweeping the road in front of a convoy. Each time we changed a technique, they adapted their TTPs. We had to always stay ahead and constantly changed up our plans. They meant business. They did not offer second chances with IEDs. Never be in a rush. Check every likely IED site, even if it means wet boots every day. Don't let timelines control your patrol. There is no timeline for success. With this, keep in mind that not every person digging next to a road is putting in an IED. Sometimes they are putting in homemade power lines or irrigating their fields to grow crops. They are helping themselves. Approach every situation with caution, but you must have PID!

- Taliban are great at sneaking in weapons and hiding them. Check everything, and let nothing go unsearched. In doing so, be respectful of the Pashtu culture, and respect women and elders. Search them when you can and if you can. Kids are your greatest source of information. Get them on your side. Don't get too complacent and let your guard down around them. Stay professional so the enemy doesn't see a weakness in us. Know when to keep your distance, and when it is okay to let them get close. They feel safe when Marines are around, and they will come up to you in bunches. This is not the time to point your weapon and utilize "shout, shove, show, shoot" methods. This is the time to build trust and protect them. Offer them candy, snacks, pens, paper, or any other small gift that they will cherish.

- During the poppy season, fighting seemed to slow down. After the harvest, around April or May, it picked up again. I guess you could say more drugs, more money, and more weapons. Many reports from other units, and even some within our battalion, said that 25mm is a favorite as are 105mm and 125mm rockets. Their IDF is subpar. We experienced no IDF, but many AA reports claim this was true. They did have these rockets, and they did use them. In our particular company AO, they did not.

- The summer heat was high! It reached 145 degrees at one point, but it stayed a constant 130 from late June until the middle of August. When we entered the cornfields, it easily added another five to ten degrees, not including the extra heat from all the gear. It started to cool down around October and got to the low teens by the middle of November. During the corn season, once it reached five feet plus, the IEDs picked up. The corn, which often reached up to ten feet or more, provided a perfect place to hide. Make sure you go into the corn. Several weapons caches were found in the cornfields. They are muddy and buggy, and they suck. But if we could take one weapon off the streets, it was a good thing. Besides, walking through the cornfields made for good conversation starters.

- I prefer to walk/patrol. When I was inside a vehicle, it felt too dangerous—too many IEDs, I guess. I had more control over my AO and my surroundings when I was on foot. Besides, it provided a great opportunity to get out and talk to the locals. I preferred that to riding around, isolating myself from the population.

- Know your first aid, and always have a combat lifesaver or doctor on your patrols. They will save your life. Know how to stop all bleeding and how to apply a tourniquet. In some cases, the best medicine is bullets downrange. I can't stress this enough. First aid is a must. It needs to be practiced over and over and over again. Then practice it some more. I don't believe that all gear should look the same, but I do believe that every Marine should have an IFAK in the same place. We train a lot in order to achieve muscle memory, and that is exactly what will be needed when an emergency situation arises. You don't have time to be indecisive.

- There were no snipers in our AO, and if there were, they did not engage us. They may use spotters—but not in the conventional sense that we think of. There were reports of suicide bombers, but we never saw them. Also, we heard reports of the enemy faking injuries, covering themselves with goat blood, drawing in coalition forces, and blowing themselves up. Fake accidents and fake car crashes are clever. Approach all accidents and injured local nationals with caution. Always have an "oh shit" plan. I think the main reason why they used this method was their ability to watch us and adapt to what we practiced.

- Know basic Pashtu and Dari. It will get you very far. Use a terp if you have one. If not, use your foreign-language-speaking Marines. When using a terp, do not allow the terp to lead or carry off with the conversation. Short sentences work best. Always look the LN you are talking to in the eyes. Don't talk through the terp—just use him. Get your Marines to Pashtu schools, classes, and courses. It is a tremendous benefit. Most of the times, the terps want to be there. If not, they would not have signed up for the job. Work with them, and teach them what you want them to know. They may be scared—or even fearful—at first. They are afraid of being seen by the Taliban, being killed, or upsetting the LNs. Remember that it is their country. Help Afghans learn English. You'll learn Pashto in the process and become a more capable counterinsurgent.

- ANA and ANP need our help. Teach them, work with them, and live with them. Share ideas, thoughts, and tactics—and understand how they operate just as they should understand how we operate. I wouldn't trust my life in their hands, but remember that they are only as good as we make them. It seemed that about half the ANA we worked with understood basic English even though they might not speak it. Don't put them down or call them names. They understand what is going on. The purpose is to work with them—not make them our enemies. Be patient, and train them every day. They will work their butts off for you. Develop a PT program for them. They will work out with you. Ensure that you are partnering at the lowest level. Incorporate ANA and ANP into your daily routine. It is good practice to have ANSF enter compounds and buildings first. Have them be the first people local nationals meet when approaching checkpoints or searching them. You can't search every trailer, but search enough to keep the enemy forces from moving things on the roads. Search as much as you can. Encourage positive ANSF interaction with the people in order to build trust between them, and have them pass out IO flyers. It is always a good idea to stay around and answer any IO questions. Share meals with the Afghans you work with as often as possible. Every day is acceptable. Treat ANSF casualties just as we do our own because they are our brothers in arms as well.

- Never take the same route, use the same formation, or set a pattern. Be unpredictable, and always assume you are being watched. Because they are watching and learning. The enemy is smart, and they understand how we operate. They will adapt their style of fighting as we adapt ours, and just as we make changes to our TTPs, they are doing the same. They are trying to stay abreast of us.

- 6-5 or 3-11 style patrolling is good, and you can never practice it enough. Patrolling needs to be practiced again and again. Team leaders should be able to lead a patrol as squad leaders, and the lowest private should be able to lead a team as his team leader does. But you must incorporate bounding over watch and satellite patrolling, which will help you open up in fields. Keep one team stationary to provide security while another team moves forward. There are many different ways to accomplish this method. Use the terrain to your advantage. Use tree lines to mask movement. Spread out when possible. Bounding works well and takes less energy, especially when it is 130 degrees.

- Know your combat-reporting procedures! IED, LZ Brief, CASEVAC (with MIST) and CFF were the most frequently used. Keep cheat sheets on you and practice, practice, rehearse, and rehearse! Incorporate these and other combat reports into all of your training, and continuously keep up on them. It should be a skill, not a trait.

- QRF! Quick Reaction Force is just that. A unit that is ready at all times to aid in the assistance of the operating unit serves a purpose to provide assistance in a timely manner.

Just because a firefight breaks out does not qualify a reason to call for QRF. All that does is waste a resource and creates an even better opportunity for the enemy to attack us. Several situations came to be where QRF was called—not at the request of the operating unit—but by the COC, and it caused too many Marines in one area. I guess one could disagree and say that you can never have too much security. Although true, you can have too many Marines in one area. A sector of fire or area can be covered quite well by one individual. Just don't overdo it; use QRF as needed, not as wanted.

- For gear and equipment, we used the standard plate carrier instead of the MTV. The MTV was bulky and caused a lot of problems restricting freedom of movement. It was difficult to reach across your body or to your back to grab something. It also weighed more than the plate carrier. Then adding in the front, back, and side SAPI plates with a basic combat load, you can have as much as sixty pounds just in the vest. The plate carriers were a huge success on foot and moving around. They weighed less, and we were able to reach around to grab whatever gear you needed. As for the SAPI plates, I didn't mind having the side ones. Some don't like them, but others do. Most of the injuries come head-on or from the back, and not many deaths—if any that I can think of—have resulted from not having the side SAPIs in. I would rather have them and not need them than need them and not have them. They do rub into the hips a lot. Mine got pretty sore on the initial push, and after the first twenty-four hours, I was on my knees in pain. You just have to adjust them to how you want them, and this kept changing for me. It took several weeks to get them exactly how I wanted them. I went from having all my gear on a belt to keep the weight off my shoulders to not even using a belt at all; everything was attached to my vest. In the end, that worked best for me. I think gear should be shooter's preference with exceptions to maybe the IFAK. Drop holsters and other leg holsters in my opinion look cool, but I would hate to have that around my leg for seven months, walking day after day, and mile after mile. I would imagine it would cause some discomfort. The standard load for a M16/M4 carrier was five thirty-round magazines, one grenade, one smoke, one pen flare, the camel back, and other items. M203 grenadiers carried about ten 40mm rounds on them, and M249 SAW gunners carried five hundred rounds, two two-hundred-round drums, and an extra hundred rounds. Some carried more, but I would recommend never carrying less. You don't need much to fight. Most of our gear stayed packed in seabags. Keep your gear clean and organized. Always have a reason for why you set your gear up.

- The IED-sniffing dogs were an amazing asset. When I found out we were getting dogs, I was skeptical about how they were going to be utilized. I kept thinking about how Marines patrol the rates of speed we can move and the long distances we covered without stopping. Plus, with the 140-degree heat, I was wondering how a dog could even survive in Afghanistan. The dogs were used to sniff out TNT and other types of homemade explosives (HME) that were commonly used by Afghan fighters. The dog was only as good as his trainer. We had some dogs that never found a single IED, and others found multiple devices. The use of the dogs when clearing roads was vital. Using V-Sweepers, metal detectors (metal detectors require practice, but it is necessary practice), and the dog gave us multiple ways to defeat the IED threat.

- I don't really have a lot to say about the use of vehicles because I never spent too much time in them. Due to the canals and the irrigation, the use of vehicles was pretty limited. Afghan roads are not roads in the traditional sense. Be prepared for them to collapse. Practice recoveries. If you set a pattern, they adapt to it really fast—and you will get hit with IEDs. If you fail to use V-Sweepers and have nobody on foot, you will get hit with IEDs. When traveling long distances, it is understandable not to have someone on foot. In choke points or areas that require you to slow down, do so. Most roads really don't allow anyone to drive faster than ten miles per hour (some may even argue five). Both are reasonable. You shouldn't be in such a hurry that you can't accurately scout your AO while driving. Be able to recognize areas that would be good places to put IEDs. I preferred to patrol rather than ride in a vehicle. I felt safer. Ensure that your ECMs work, and know how to troubleshoot. Blue Force Tracker (BFT) is a good means of C2 or your command and control techniques. Ensure you have Marines that understand how to operate it.

- For combat reporting, basic combat reporting formats worked well. Position reports (POSREPS), situation reports (SITREPS), and contact reports are the basic ones. There were many other reports that were used. It is important to send these reports in as needed, when needed. The better the COC can track your movement and location, the better off you both are. Although it can get frustrating to keep updating your POSREP, it is worth the extra hassle in the end. After all, command and control is vital on the battlefield.

- PCCs and PCIs work. You must do them by the number. The squad leader or patrol leader must not look past this. Each patrol is different, and each mission is different. All gear has to be checked prior to leaving the COP. Again, you must do them by the numbers. Establish a standard checklist that covers personnel, gear, equipment, weapons, pyro, smoke, radios, PPE, and mission information. Leave room for any last-minute questions. Brief the orders process, and don't leave out any information. As time goes on, certain things may be omitted, such as terrain or weather since they are pretty much self-explanatory. The first three paragraphs are vital. The fourth and fifth are important but don't have to be so detailed. Ensure you have a corpsmen, or a combat lifesaver, ensure you have a medevac plan and a lost Marine plan. These are just some basics, but each mission will be different. I was successful with using a map and a GPS. I used the compass more at night, but as you get to know your AO, it is pretty much all done by map. Remember that PCCs are physical (gear, equipment, etc.) and PCIs are mental (mission, tasks, PIR, CCIRs, etc.).

Talking Points

1) We are here in your village at the request of your government to help your brave security forces restore security and prosperity.

2) We are in partnership with your own security forces. Together we can restore peace and prosperity to your village.

3) We seek your assistance in identifying those who are seeking to destroy your government and keep you in fear. The sooner we can identify these enemies of _____, the sooner we can remove them from your village.

4) Coalition forces have no intention to stay in your village permanently. We will stay long enough to restore security and will leave when your own security forces can provide this security on their own.

5) We look upon you as friends. We have left our families to assist you in your struggles, just as we would for any friend.

Things to Report

1) Any missing or captured US personnel and/or sensitive equipment

2) Death or injury of any US personnel, other CFs, HVIs, key leaders, LNs, or enemies

3) Any EOF incident

4) Complete loss of communication for more than one hour with friendly or any adjacent units

5) Any situation that requires QRF

6) Any fratricide

7) Violations of laws of war, including detainee abuse

8) Any mosque incidents

9) Use of pyro or ammo, including warning shots, or shooting dogs to protect mission or personnel

10) Permission from company commander to detain any person of interest, sheiks, imams, or anyone under the age of eighteen

5-3-5 Rules

PCC/PCI	Guardian Angel	No better friend, no worse enemy
Rehearsals	Geometry of Fires	First do no harm. They are not our enemy, but the enemy hides among them.
Confirmation Briefs	Unity of Command	You have to look at these people as if they are trying to kill you, but you can't treat them that way.
AAR		Be polite, be professional, have a plan to kill everyone you meet. Sturdy professionalism
Debrief		Make yourself hard to kill

Know and understand that the Afghan people are not our enemy, but our enemy hides among them. Don't be afraid to use "wave" tactics. Wave at everyone you see. It gets them to look in your direction so you can recognize targets. Greet people by saying *salaam* (peace). Treat them with the same manners you would want your family to be treated with. Trust no one. Never let your guard down. Act like a cop; treat everyone with respect, regardless of how they act or what they have done. Respect is everything in Afghan culture; don't create more enemies by disrespecting some. Always be prepared to go kinetic—no matter how secure the situation seems.

Good luck, keep your head up, eyes open, button up your chin strap, and suck it up! Get some!

TRUE DIRECTIONS
AN AFFILIATE OF TARCHER BOOKS

OUR MISSION

Tarcher's mission has always been to publish books
that contain great ideas. Why? Because:

GREAT LIVES BEGIN WITH GREAT IDEAS

At Tarcher, we recognize that many talented authors, speakers, educators,
and thought-leaders share this mission and deserve to be published
– many more than Tarcher can reasonably publish ourselves. True
Directions is ideal for authors and books that increase awareness, raise
consciousness, and inspire others to live their ideals and passions.

Like Tarcher, True Directions books are designed to do three things:
inspire, inform, and motivate.

Thus, True Directions is an ideal way for these important voices to
bring their messages of hope, healing, and help to the world.

Every book published by True Directions– whether it is non-
fiction, memoir, novel, poetry or children's book – continues
Tarcher's mission to publish works that bring positive change
in the world. We invite you to join our mission.

For more information, see the True Directions website:
www.iUniverse.com/TrueDirections/SignUp

Be a part of Tarcher's community to bring positive change in this world!
See exclusive author videos, discover new and exciting books, learn about
upcoming events, connect with author blogs and websites, and more!
WWW.TARCHERBOOKS.COM

TRUE DIRECTIONS
AN AFFILIATE OF TARCHER BOOKS

Lightning Source UK Ltd.
Milton Keynes UK
UKOW04f2249030316

269542UK00001B/131/P